THINK BIG! AN ENTREPRENEUR'S GUIDE TO PARTNERING WITH LARGE COMPANIES

Les Pardew and Brant Slade

COURSE TECHNOLOGY
CENGAGE Learning™

Australia, Brazil, Japan, Korea, Mexico, Singapore, Spain, United Kingdom, United States

COURSE TECHNOLOGY
CENGAGE Learning™

Think BIG! An Entrepreneur's Guide to Partnering with Large Companies
Les Pardew and Brant Slade

Publisher and General Manager, Course Technology PTR:
Stacy L. Hiquet

Associate Director of Marketing:
Sarah Panella

Manager of Editorial Services:
Heather Talbot

Marketing Manager:
Mark Hughes

Acquisitions Editor:
Mitzi Koontz

Project Editor:
Sandy Doell

Editorial Services Coordinator:
Jen Blaney

Copy Editor:
Heather Urschel

Interior Layout Tech:
Bill Hartman

Cover Designer:
Luke Fletcher

Indexer:
Katherine Stimson

Proofreader:
Sandi Wilson

For product information and technology assistance, contact us at **Cengage Learning Customer & Sales Support, 1-800-354-9706**

For permission to use material from this text or product, submit all requests online at **cengage.com/permissions**. Further permissions questions can be e-mailed to **permissionrequest@cengage.com**.

Library of Congress Control Number: 2009933316

ISBN-13: 978-1-4354-5475-0

ISBN-10: 1-4354-5475-8

Course Technology, a part of Cengage Learning
20 Channel Center Street
Boston, MA 02210
USA

Cengage Learning is a leading provider of customized learning solutions with office locations around the globe, including Singapore, the United Kingdom, Australia, Mexico, Brazil, and Japan. Locate your local office at: **international.cengage.com/region**.

Cengage Learning products are represented in Canada by Nelson Education, Ltd.

For your lifelong learning solutions, visit **courseptr.com**.

Printed in Canada
1 2 3 4 5 6 7 11 10 09

THINK BIG! AN ENTREPRENEUR'S GUIDE TO PARTNERING WITH LARGE COMPANIES

Les Pardew and Brant Slade

About the Authors

Les Pardew is a lifelong entrepreneur. He has founded several companies and developed a number of products by partnering with larger companies.

Les is a veteran of the video game and entertainment industry completing more than 150 video game titles. He started his career in video games in 1987 doing animation for *Magic Johnson Fast Break Basketball* for the Commodore 64. He went on to create art for several major games including *Robin Hood Prince of Thieves, Star Wars, Wrestle Mania, NCAA Basketball, Stanley Cup Hockey, Jack Nicholas Golf,* and *Where in the World/USA is Carmen Sandiego* to name a few. He is an avid artist and still creates art for some of the video games his companies create.

He was the founder of Saffire, one of the industry's preeminent game developers. He built the company from humble beginnings in his basement to a thriving group of more than 120 programmers, artists, musicians, and other creative people. In 1995, Saffire was named by *Entrepreneur Magazine* as one of America's hottest new companies, and in 1999, it was 32 on the Utah 100 list of the state's fastest growing companies.

Les lives in Utah with his wife and family. He is the father of five children and grandfather of four grandchildren.

Brant Slade is a Managing Partner and Chief Executive Officer of Operational Results, Inc. As a consultant and educator he has assisted a wide variety of companies, including many from the Fortune 500, in their drive for continuous improvement and world-class excellence. His client list includes: Apple Computers, Caterpillar, Coca-Cola, Dial, Dole Fruits and Vegetables, Ernest & Julio Gallo Wineries, Fujitsu, General Nutrition, Giant Foods, Heinz, Henkel, Honeywell, Huntsman Chemical, Jockey, Kellogg's, Kimberly Clark, Kodak, LTV Steel, Malt-O-Meal, Marshall, M&M Mars, Monsanto, Nabisco, Nynex, Pioneer, Procter & Gamble, PPG, Sara Lee, Smith Kline Beecham, and many others. A number of his clients have achieved Class A recognition. Collectively, his clients have documented savings of more than a billion dollars while under Brant's guidance. One multi-national client delivered over $350 million in savings while Brant operated as the Managing Partner for their company.

Prior to founding Operational Results, Inc. Brant was a Managing Partner and member of the Board of Directors at The Oliver Wight Companies. He was a Principal with Oliver Wight for more than 15 years. Prior to becoming a consultant, Brant had significant experience in industry where he has held positions of General Manager, Supply Chain Director, and Materials Manager. He has a strong process and consumer products industry background, and he is proficient in the integration of manufacturing and distribution functions. He is a noted expert in Operational Strategy, Supply Chain Integration, and Sales and Operations Planning.

Brant has instructed numerous courses on Strategic Planning, Business Management, Sales and Operations Planning, Demand Management, and Supply Chain Management. He is a frequent speaker for various professional organizations. He has served as a Board Member of the Supply Chain Council and was the Conference Chair at the 1999 Supply Chain World Wide Conference and Exposition in Chicago, Illinois. Brant holds undergraduate and graduate degrees from Brigham Young University, and he is certified at the fellow level with the American Production and Inventory Control Society (APICS).

Contents

Chapter 1

Why Partner?

Occasionally you will hear a report of a small business that overcame the odds and succeeded where many others had failed. Even less often you will hear reports of how a mega corporation grew from a humble small beginning. The important thing to note here is that both of these are news; this fact by itself shows how uncommon it is to succeed and really grow a small business into a large business.

While it is true that all large companies have to start somewhere, most of these companies gained success and continue to be successful because they are adept at forming and maintaining good partnerships with other companies. In our current global economy, there are very few opportunities for companies to grow to any substantial size without partnering with other companies along the way. Large corporations form partnerships with other companies both large and small all the time. For the small business owner, a good partnership with a large company can have a tremendous impact on the small business' success.

In this chapter we will examine some of the reasons why small businesses should partner with larger companies. We will first take a look at what larger companies have to offer and then use that list to help you identify the areas where a partnership could be beneficial to your company. We will finish the chapter with some examples of successful partnerships that had a positive impact on the smaller company.

In business, size really does matter. Larger companies have many advantages in a marketplace. Some of these advantages are as follows:

- Money
- Markets
- Expertise
- Distribution
- Name recognition

Money

Before I had my first job, my budget and spending practices centered on just a few dollars a week. My income was low, so my spending also had to be low. After I started working on a regular basis, though, the whole economy around how I received and spent money changed dramatically. I had a much larger budget to deal with and by virtue of that, I also had more opportunities. There is a similar difference in scale between economies surrounding small companies and those associated with larger companies.

As a small business owner, you might feel good about revenue and expenses running a few hundred thousand dollars a month. A large cooperation, on the other hand, may routinely deal with several hundred million dollars a month in revenue and expenses. Because large corporations have to deal with funds on a massive scale, they also have to have massive amounts of money available to them in either cash reserves or lines of credit. Like you, these large companies have to spend a significant amount of time and effort to maintain sufficient capital to ensure the company can meet its target growth strategy. The primary difference between the large company and a small business is the scale at which the capitol is maintained.

One of the most difficult tasks of a small business owner is obtaining sufficient amounts of capitol to fund the expansion and growth of the company. Larger companies have usually been around longer and have already established sources of capitol. This means that the larger company may have money available to fund a small partner who fits into its overall company objectives. Financing from a large corporate partner can also bring with it much better terms than those that are available to the small business owner through other methods like banks or investors.

Because larger companies have to deal with funds on a much larger scale, they also have to look at their markets very differently than a small company. They usually are interested in large lucrative markets with massive revenue potential. Often large lucrative markets have multiple smaller specialized parts that are either too small or too specialized for the larger company to address effectively. In these situations, partnering with a small company with expertise in one component of the market can lead to the big company having access to the larger overall market. (In Chapters 2 and 4 we will cover how you can determine whether your company can find a good place in the overall objectives of potential partner companies.)

Financial support from a large company can take many forms, including the following:

- Revenue
- Investment
- Purchase

Revenue

One of the most common and best ways that a large company can partner with a smaller company is for the larger company to pay the smaller company for goods or services. In other words, the larger company becomes a client of the smaller company, thus increasing the smaller company's revenue by increasing its sales.

The nice part about a supplier/client relationship for the small business is that because all of the inflow of cash is revenue, there is no restriction on how it is spent and no obligation to pay the money back at any time in the future. Revenue-based relationships are just an extension of normal company business.

The downside to the revenue-based model is that there is no long term commitment between the parties unless a specific contract is entered into, and relationships of this nature can change at any moment based on market pressure. A smaller company may have to scale up production or add employees to handle the additional workload, so if the larger company decides to change suppliers, the smaller company is left holding the bag.

As mentioned above, one way to make revenue-based relationships more reliable is to enter into a contract for supplying the goods or services for a specific amount of time. The smaller company can then plan for changes in workload based on the contracts. Contract extensions are also a possibility for helping the small business owner plan for the future. It is a lot easier to negotiate a contract extension than it is to wake up one morning to find your largest client just moved its business to one of your competitors.

A good example of revenue-based systems is in the video game industry. Over the last decade, video games have grown into a significant industry with several game publishers reporting revenue over a billion dollars. Some of these companies are household names, including Nintendo, Microsoft, Sony, Electronic Arts (EA), and Activision. While almost all major video game publishers maintain in-house development studios, there are a large number of games published every year that are created by small independent development studios.

The difference in size and scale between the large publisher and the small developer can be staggering. On one hand you have a massive, multi-billion dollar organization, while on the other the development group may only be a couple of guys working out of a single office. The partnership between large publishers and small developers is a long-standing tradition in the video game industry, however. There are many good reasons for these partnerships.

Video game design, by its very nature, requires a great deal of creativity and specialized knowledge. Often the best place to find the knowledge and creativity for new and better games is not in a large, in-house development studio that requires an extensive amount of structure and accountability to operate effectively. Creativity and specialized knowledge are generally much better cultivated in smaller organizations.

Another more common reason large publishers might want to use a small developer is to contain costs. In-house development studios are very expensive to operate mainly because they require so many highly skilled—and therefore expensive—personnel. They are impractical to maintain unless the game title the team is working on has significant upside potential. Therefore, many of the smaller game titles that might not support the expenses involved in an in-house operation are usually farmed out to independent teams for a fixed development cost.

Having a large contingent of smaller independent development studios available to large publishers creates a certain amount of flexibility. Publishers can scale production up or down without having to deal with big swings in the number of employees working for them. This flexibility can be very important in a fast-paced competitive industry.

Small developers often have great game ideas but very limited resources to bring these ideas to market. By partnering with a large publisher, they can gain market access that they couldn't get on their own. They also can get additional funding to help them complete their game. The publisher benefits from the standpoint that they get to review numerous game ideas and choose those with the most potential.

For the small game developer, the chance to partner with a large game publisher often means a work contract that can be anywhere from six months to two years of work. Contracts can range in value from a few hundred thousand dollars to several million dollars. Locking in a contract with a large publisher can mean steady work and stability for the small developer.

Another advantage for the small developer is that the only likely exit strategy for a video game developer is to be hired by a publisher. In actuality, a proven development team with a strong track record is very attractive to a publisher as opposed to trying to build one itself.

For an efficient, well managed video game developer, contracting with the large publisher can help the team have immediate and regular cash flow while it develops its own technology. It also gives the team a chance to learn to work together and produce high quality product without the need for outside investors.

The video game industry is not the only industry where there are numerous smaller companies partnering with larger firms. Almost any industry that relies on the talents or skill of individuals to produce its products is likely to have many good opportunities for smaller businesses to partner with larger companies. Some other examples are the motion picture industry, construction, agriculture, consulting, music, and design. If your company is in an industry that relies heavily on human capital to get the job done, you likely will have a very good chance to gain revenue funding for your company.

Investments

When a large company invests in a smaller company, meaning it buys a portion of the smaller company and becomes a part owner, it is usually for a very different reason than why a private investor or venture capital firm might invest. Usually large companies make investments for strategic reasons rather than a monetary return. For example, a large paper company may invest in a lumber company to ensure a steady supply of raw materials. An electronics company may invest in a chain of retail stores to ensure favorable access to the market. A shipping company might invest in a software company that specializes in tracking packages to add to their company's offerings to customers. A strategic investment like those just mentioned helps the larger companies gain an advantage in the marketplace.

These types of investments can range from a small minority share of a company all the way up to a full acquisition. A minority investment in a smaller company typically means that the larger company has no real interest in running the smaller company or adding them to their subsidiary pool, but rather is more interested in ensuring a vital partner's financial health and viability. The smaller investment may come with specific preferential treatment for the larger company, or it might come with a stipulation that the larger company maintains a seat on the board of directors to ensure that the larger company's interests are represented.

If you are interested in finding an investment from a larger company for your business, you first need to understand what your company has to offer the larger company and identify why it would be a good idea for it to invest in your company. Sometimes the reasons might be obvious, like the paper mill investing in a lumber company, but often the investment interest of the larger company is spawned by the larger company's desire to move in a new direction, so it may not be readily apparent. Just because you might not be privy to the inner workings of the larger company, though, doesn't mean you can't find out what companies you might partner with. A little common sense and a clear understanding of your industry will go a long way to help you target potential partners.

A good way to understand what companies might consider an investment in your company is to map your industry's supply chain and then find your company's place in that chain. Your best opportunity for investment will be the companies on either side of yours in the supply chain.

Let's say your company's primary product is a software package that helps construction companies estimate project costs. You can determine your place in the supply chain by looking at who pays you and who you pay. Construction companies buy your software, so they are above you in the supply chain. Part of your software is licensed from a software research company and you pay them for the license. The software research company is below you in the supply chain. The construction company might be interested in investing in your company to have you supply custom software to them for specific building projects, thus giving them a competitive advantage over their competition. The software research firm might invest in your company to help you expand your market and thus increase their own sales.

An investment in your company can be beneficial in many ways, but there are potential problems with such investments as well. For one thing, you are bringing in a new owner who may have objectives and goals that may not always be in line with the best interests of your company. Say, for instance, one of your company goals is to take the company public. Your investment partner might not think that is a good idea. When looking at an investment from another company, particularly a larger company, you should be very clear with each other about the goals of both parties.

Another problem that might surface with investors is that often investors are unfamiliar with your industry and may not understand how things work. Sometimes what seems like a normal or typical problem that you routinely deal with may seem like a huge issue to an investor. It is difficult to deal with panicked investors stealing valuable time from your business.

Most investors invest to gain a return on their money. Sometimes their interests don't always coincide with the best interests of the company. For example, an investor may want to take a buyout offer that you know is a bad deal because the company willing to purchase your company may just want to shut your company down to eliminate competition. The investor just wants the money. They may not be concerned that the deal leaves you without a company or a job.

Having an investor isn't necessarily bad but you do need to be careful that the investor is the right fit for you company. As attractive as the money might look, don't just do the deal because you are strapped for cash.

Purchase

The purchase of a company is very similar to an investment in a company with the exception that the larger company is looking to control the smaller company. In the case of investments of 50% or more, the larger company is essentially trying to expand its operations into the area currently occupied by the smaller company—the larger company is looking for a way to expand its products or services into areas that are currently being serviced by the smaller company. For example, a large software company that sells custom software to the legal profession may purchase a company that creates web-based applications to buy expertise in that area. The rationale might be that instead of creating its own development group to migrate its software to the internet, it is more cost effective and faster to buy a company that already produces web applications and have it take over the development efforts.

A purchase is the ultimate partnership relationship. It is a complete commitment by both parties to work together.

In a purchase, the ongoing cash needs of the smaller purchased company become an operational budget item of the larger purchasing company. This type of financial support has the potential to supply the purchased company with the resources and time it needs to fully develop its product line and expand its market.

Markets

Partnering with a large company can give your company better access to your market. Larger companies already have established channels through which they sell their products. By partnering with a larger company, you may be able to take advantage of its market access with your own products.

By definition, a company's market are those companies or individuals that buy directly from that company; however, when thinking of markets it is often best to think of them in terms of the ultimate purchase. For example, a book publisher generally does not sell its books directly to book readers. It sells its books to book stores and other book retailers, and those stores sell the books to the readers. In this case, the book retailer is the publisher's direct market but the readers are its ultimate market. While a small publisher may have books that are popular with its readers, it may have problems getting book retailers to carry the books because of its limited offering and size.

For a book retailer, one meeting with a large publisher can result in hundreds of titles, while a meeting with a small publisher might only result in a handful of books. The retailer needs to ensure that it has a full store, so it will obviously look to the larger publishers first. The larger publishers have likely already formed partnerships with the book retailers where they supply a certain number of titles on a regular basis. They also already have strong access to the reader market. By partnering with the larger publisher, a small publisher can, in essence, gain the same market advantage that the large publisher already enjoys. The small publisher will likely have to pay a percentage of sales to the large publisher partner, but the market access will give the small publisher a chance to sell its books to a much larger market. The large publisher partnering with the small publisher increases the size of its catalog and also helps to fill its title quota, which might be in jeopardy because of authors missing their deadlines, for example.

A very important aspect of any market for a product or service is to create a demand for that product or service. It doesn't matter if a company has a great product if no one knows about it. More often than not it isn't the best product that has the highest sales in a given market, but rather the best known product in that market. Large companies spend billions of dollars a year to market and promote their products. They have vast marketing departments devoted to making their products the first thing a person thinks of when making a purchasing decision.

Creating demand for a product or service takes considerable resources—often more than the cost of developing the product or service in the first place. First the public needs to be made aware of the product through an aggressive mix of advertising and public relations. These efforts may include such things as television, print, radio, and internet advertising, guest or celebrity appearances on television and radio shows, product placement in movies or video games, in-store demonstrations, product giveaways, and the list goes on and on. It takes a lot of resources and money to effectively execute a marketing campaign on a national or international level. It also takes a lot of specialized knowledge.

The marketing groups at many large companies have very sophisticated systems for tracking and predicting the effectiveness of advertising efforts. Because the stakes are so high and the amounts of money devoted to marketing are so big, these groups go to great efforts to understand their markets and target their approach specifically to their customers. Wherever possible they try to tie every dollar spent on promotion back to sales in as specific a manner as possible. This information is then used to refine and polish the marketing approach for even better effectiveness.

The majority of smaller companies don't have the vast resources available to them that a large company has for putting together effective marketing campaigns. Usually tier marketing budgets are much smaller and their reach into the market is limited. By partnering with a large company, a small business can take advantage of the marketing resources of the large company to increase its product or service presence in the market.

For some small companies the large company isn't so much access to a market; the large company *is* the market. For example, a company that converts gasoline and diesel motors to run on natural gas could have a nice little business doing one-off conversions for individual consumers. On the other hand, one partnership with a major shipping company with a fleet of thousands of vehicles could catapult that little company into something huge. In this case, the large company becomes the smaller company's primary market. In this type of relationship, the large company isn't interested in marketing the smaller company's service; it is interested in using the service to enhance its own operation. The smaller company provides a way for the larger company to cut expenses and improve the lifespan of its fleet.

Expertise

Sometimes the most important benefit of a good partnership with a large company is the knowledge that company has to offer. The larger company may have knowledge of specialized manufacturing techniques. It may have a strong understanding of the market. It may have a research and development department that can take on special projects. It may have political connections.

In business knowledge is power. For example, a streamlined and efficient market delivery system can mean less money spent on shipping and larger margins or a lower price than competitors. Wal-Mart has invested significantly in its product tracking and management system. Its system is optimized to the point that it has a cost advantage over its competitors for the same product offering. Even though the difference between Wal-Mart and its nearest competitor is probably only one percent, that one percent still translates into lower prices in the store for the majority of its products.

Some companies, such as General Electric, have integrated employee training programs that keep their employees up to date in the latest technologies, management methods, and other important company information. Their programs include on-the-job training programs and online training as well. They also go a step further and have created a centralized training facility that is similar to a mini-university where they bring employees for intensive training programs. They cover almost every aspect of business and human development in their courses.

The most important expertise to any small company is the knowledge that can solve the current company problems. The majority of the problems that face small companies, however, are not unique. Chances are pretty high that those very problems have been faced before by other companies. There is a good chance that the very problems you are facing now were faced and overcome by many of your potential partner companies. Gaining information that solves current company dilemmas could very well be more important to your company than any other benefit you might gain from the partnership.

One of the places where expertise might benefit your company is in research and development. Large companies expend significant efforts to develop new products. This is especially true for companies who rely on cutting edge technology as a competitive advantage. They can spend the time and money to fully research new product ideas and test them for the market. As a partner company, you may be able to take advantage of their R&D departments to perfect your current products, thereby helping to avoid costly mistakes when you are ready to take your products to market.

Distribution

Large companies usually have a strong channel to distribute their products to the market. Consider a large consumer product company like Proctor and Gamble. It maintains a strong presence in stores throughout the world; it has shelf space in most major retailers and a distribution system to put its products on those shelves; it has a network of people to ensure that the flow of products through the system is consistent. In essence, it has access to its market. If you have a small consumer product company, you likely don't have anything near the breadth and scope of what Proctor and Gamble has. What would happen if your product had the same access to the market as Proctor and Gamble?

In addition to expanding a company's current market, partnering with a large company can also give the small company distribution access to new markets or territories. For example, consider the case of a flour mill that sells primarily to a regional market but develops some muffin mixes that could have nationwide appeal. Rather than taking its one food offering to all of the grocery stores across the nation, it would only take one trip to a large company like General Mills to form a partnership and gain access to a nationwide market through General Mills global distribution.

Distribution is a lot more than just the warehousing and shipping of your products, though; there are any number of warehouse/distribution companies that will do that for a fee. Distribution is also the relationships with retailers or other end sellers of your product or service. A good relationship with the person who ultimately sells your product to its end consumer is critical to the ultimate success of your product in the marketplace. A friend of mine is a *New York Times* best selling author. His books sell all across the nation, but they sell particularly well in Texas. The reason they sell so well in Texas is because of a regional book representative of the publisher. This book rep is a big fan of my friend's work. Because he likes his work so much, he told every book store he visited how good the books were. On his recommendation many of the bookstore owners read his books and they also liked them and recommended them to their customers. My friend sells a lot more books in Texas than any other area in the country all because of this one book rep.

Large companies often have representatives who have long-standing relationships with retailers. These relationships are hard to duplicate because they've been built up over a number of years. By partnering with a large company that already has close relationships with retailers, your products stand a much better chance of making it to the store shelves than if you were to try to develop those relationships yourself.

Small companies often struggle to gain access to their market. If they decide to gain direct access to that market, they then have the huge task of developing a sales and distribution system. Not only are sales and distribution systems expensive, they may not be the core competency of the small company. A good partnership with a large company that already has access to the market can allow the smaller company to focus on its core business expertise while increasing its market.

Name Recognition

One big advantage that large companies have over small companies is name recognition. All things being equal, people will generally buy a product from someone they know. All things not being equal, they will still buy a product from someone they know.

It is human nature to build relationships. We build relationships with other humans. We build relationships with pets and animals. We even build relationships with objects. For example, have you ever caught yourself or someone you know talking to their car or computer? Do you have trouble throwing out an old pair of shoes or some other article of clothing because of a bond you have developed with it? Companies know this tendency and they try to exploit it as much as possible. It is called relationship marketing and it is extremely effective.

Relationship marketing is a process of creating a relationship between a company and its products or services and its clients. It is a combination of giving clients or customers a reliable product that they can trust and offering effective customer service. It is also a part of what is called brand management.

Brand management refers to the establishment and support devoted to developing a brand. When talking about a brand, we are not talking about an identifying mark on cattle, but rather we are referring to a named product, product line, or service. Brands are used by companies to distinguish their products from other similar products. They can represent a single product, such as the soft drink 7 Up, or they can designate products from a particular company, such as Ford. Brands are powerful tools for companies because they give the customer a name with which to build a relationship. They create what is known as *brand loyalty*, where a customer purchases a product or service based on their knowledge of and relationship with the brand.

Creating brands is primarily the domain of large companies because it takes so much work to establish and maintain a brand. Small companies can be successful creating a brand but usually it is in a niche market where they have direct access to the customer. National or international brand recognition for the general market is a lot more difficult to manage. By partnering with a large company that has already established a brand identity, you can take advantage of the company's name recognition without all of the overhead of brand management. You can also establish your own brand in association with theirs.

What Will Benefit My Company Most?

As outlined in this chapter, there are many benefits to partnering with a large company. However, because every company is unique, not all of the benefits may be of major importance to your company. Before you go out and seek a partnership with a big company you should take a hard look at what your company really needs. Some of the advantages stated already in this chapter are as follows:

- Money
- Markets
- Expertise
- Distribution
- Name recognition

Look closely at the preceding list and think about which item is most important to your company. If your company is already profitable and you have the capital to expand, you might not need money as much as you need access to the market. On the other hand, if your company is in need of money, is that need for money greater than your need for a larger market? Sometimes increasing sales solves the money problem. Maybe your company needs everything on the list. (What company doesn't?) It is important to rank the company's needs in order of priority because it will form the foundation of how you choose the likely companies for partnership.

You should resist the temptation to just go for the money. While money seems to always be in short supply for most small companies, it is not always the most important element for your company.

A good way to determine your priorities is to take each item on the list and walk through how things will change for your company if that issue were resolved. For example, what would change about your company if it had great name recognition for its products? How would that affect sales, marketing, distribution opportunities, manufacturing requirements, and so on? Go through the whole process. Think through the benefits and potential problems. The more thorough the process, the better prepared you will be to make a decision.

After you complete the exercise for each item on the list, compare the lists. You should be able to pick out the top priority, the next most important priority, and so forth. When you have your priorities ranked, you can then use them to help you evaluate the companies that you want to approach for a partnership opportunity. For example, if the top priority for your company is to achieve better distribution of your products, maybe you should start by researching which companies in your industry have the best distribution.

A Partnership Story

Several years ago a Wal-Mart executive had a great idea for a computer game that he thought would sell well in the hunting department. The idea was that if someone created a realistic hunting game, they could sell it to the hunters that came into the store looking for hunting gear. The reasoning was that hunters can only hunt deer a couple of weeks in a year on average, so a hunting game in which they could hunt simulated deer anytime they wanted made a lot of sense.

Wal-Mart contacted a game company, WizardWorks Software, that it regularly did business with and asked them to develop a deer-hunting game. Wal-Mart offered to buy 20,000 units up front. WizardWorks, like many other game publishers, was a little skeptical but wanted to keep Wal-Mart happy, so they in turn contacted a small developer called Sunstorm Interactive and asked them to develop the game.

The developer of the game went to work and interviewed several hunters, asking them about the hunting experience and working out how they could simulate it in a game. They created the game called *Deer Hunter.* Many in the game industry were less than impressed with the product, claiming that it wasn't a game at all. However, they were all surprised when the game began to sell in huge numbers, which no one expected. Before the end of the year, *Deer Hunter* was the number one selling game in North America and was a top 10 selling game for several years and many revisions later.

The Wal-Mart executive was right: they could sell deer-hunting games in their hunting department. In fact, not only did they sell a lot of games, they also sold a lot of computers to the hunters who needed a machine to play the game on. It was an interesting situation in which a $20 game was getting people to buy a $1,000 computer.

The partnership of a small game developer with a large game publisher with an even larger retail company was a huge success. Wal-Mart didn't know how to develop games, but they saw an opportunity and found a company that did. WizardWorks found Sunstorm Interactive and together they formed a partnership to develop the game. The partnership extended for several games thereafter as well. *Deer Hunter* and its many derivatives not only became one of the top selling computer games of all time, it also created a whole new genre of hunting games that didn't really exist before. Now there are hunting games on almost every platform, dealing with almost every kind of hunting known to man and a few that are pure fantasy.

Maybe there is a chance for your company to be like Sunstorm and create a hugely successful partnership with a large, well-known company like Wal-Mart. The only way you will find out is to get out there and see for yourself. Hopefully this book will help you to not only make a great partnership, but also do it in a way that will bring lasting rewards to both your company and your partner company.

Chapter 2

What Makes a Good Partnership?

A partnership—whether in business or one's personal life—is a serious decision and one that should never be taken lightly. The word *partnership* denotes a common purpose and requires significant cooperation. A good partnership requires a commitment from both parties to work toward a common goal that hopefully will be beneficial to both. If either party is unable or unwilling to live up to their part of the partnership, the results can be and often are disastrous.

In the previous chapter we took a look at why small companies should partner with large corporations. In this chapter we will examine the attributes necessary for a good partnership. Rather than deal with all of the things that can go wrong in partnerships, we will instead focus on the elements that are necessary to create a successful partnership. Later in Chapter 4 we will cover some of the things to be careful about when partnering with a large company.

Components of a Good Partnership

There are many factors that have to work together to make a good partnership. When these factors all come together, the possibilities of success are almost unlimited. When one or more components are weak or missing, however, the chances of success are limited. When contemplating a partnership, paying careful attention to the components of a good partnership can help you craft a truly successful future for both companies. The following list covers several of the most vital aspects of a good partnership:

- The partnership fulfills mutual need
- It takes advantage of strengths
- Both parties have compatible objectives
- The partnership is fair to both parties
- Both parties are trustworthy
- The agreement is clearly laid out and well understood by both parties
- There is a clear mechanism for ending the partnership
- Win/win: Better to walk away than to enter a bad relationship

Although the preceding list may not be complete for every situation, it contains some of the core aspects of any successful partnership. There will always be attributes that are unique to every situation and industry, and as with all of the advice presented in this book, our goal is to get you started and help you make good decisions—not make those decisions for you. Ultimately you have to evaluate your own circumstances and make the best choice you can.

Fulfilling Mutual Needs

The whole idea of a partnership is to combine work, talents, and resources to achieve a goal that would be difficult or impossible to obtain separately. This is the case with domestic partnerships and it is also the case with business partnerships. When two companies consider a partnership, they are doing so for their own benefit. The best partnerships will fulfill a mutual need for both partnering companies.

A mutual need does not mean that both companies have the same, identical need; it simply means that the partnership results in a meaningful benefit for both companies that is compatible with the purpose of the partnership. For example, one company may be looking for wider distribution of their products, while the partner company, which already has wide distribution, might be looking for a new product to put through their system. The specific goal of each company is different, but the overall goal of selling more products is very compatible with the two companies' individual goals.

The very first step in any attempt to form a partnership is to find common ground. That common ground should be the basis for the relationship. What does each company need that can be achieved if both companies work together? It is important for both parties to understand the need from the other partner's perspective so that they can go into the partnership understanding the role they play not only for their respective company but for their partner as well.

Core Business

The strongest relationships are usually those that enhance the core business of both parties. A shipping company and a mining company can make a great partnership, for example, because the mining company needs a way to get its products to its market and the shipping company needs something to haul. By forming an ongoing partnership, the shipping company is able to purchase and maintain specific types of trucks and equipment for hauling raw ore. The mining company is able to produce more ore from the mines, thereby increasing their revenue potential because they can deliver it more consistently through their relationship with the shipping company. Both parties have enhanced core business opportunities through their cooperation with the other company.

In the example above, if the shipping company didn't handle raw materials and dealt only with moving furniture, there could be some significant problems making a meaningful partnership. For one thing, the shipping company would have to obtain completely different trucks to transport ore because furniture shipping is very different from shipping raw minerals and requires different equipment. The shipping company's core business is not shipping ore; it is shipping furniture. Even though there are many similarities in shipping, they're very different businesses. The ore shipping business could be seen as a "nice to have contract" but it is not essential to their business. "Nice to have business" is not as important to a partner as core business.

When one partner is looking at their livelihood in a partnership while the other is looking at just gaining extra business, their motivating factors are very different. It is similar to the story of two riders on a tandem bicycle trying to climb a steep grade to the top of a summit. After nearly killing himself, the front biker stops to catch his breath on the top of the hill and looks back at the second biker, who hasn't even broken sweat, and exclaims, "Wow! I didn't think we were going to make it."

The second biker replies, "I didn't think we would either, but just to make sure we didn't slip back down the mountain I kept the brake on as tight as I could."

One partner in the bike ride did all of the work, while the other partner was more concerned about not going backward. The needs of the two were not aligned. The partner who relied on the partnership for their core business (the rider in front) was fully engaged in the success of the endeavor. The other partner was more concerned about not going backward and was actually hindering their progress.

Not all partnerships will have both companies' needs perfectly aligned, and some good partnerships can be maintained between two companies even if one is not totally dependent on the partnership working. In most cases, large companies have multiple business partnerships and they will not be totally dependent on any one of them, but the department or division that you work most closely with might still be very dependent on your partnership. In that case, the partnership can still succeed because the people you will work with on a daily basis are very concerned with how well your partnership works.

Take Advantage of Strengths

Every company has strengths and weaknesses. Having a clear understanding of the strengths and weaknesses of your own company and those of your potential partner will help to create a better partnership. It will help you to see how the partnership works and how it should function both contractually and functionally.

Very few companies are fully vertically self-sufficient. Even the largest companies will out-source significant amounts of their operation. Good examples of this are the plethora of payroll services, accounting firms, law firms, and other common professional organizations. These firms have become so specialized that often companies won't even think of trying to develop internal expertise. Rather, they will look for and engage experts in given fields so that they can focus their attention on their core business needs. By focusing on their own strengths and partnering with other companies whose strengths are in other necessary areas, large and small companies alike can become more efficient and better prepared to meet the challenges of the future.

Back in the mid 1980s I had an opportunity to be involved with what was then a small fledgling industry: video games. At that time, the graphic power of computers was very weak and creating art for the games was somewhat specialized. There were no schools teaching artists how to make art for games. Because I had a chance to work on some of the games from the beginning, I gained some experience in creating art. I also noticed that most game developers were having trouble finding qualified artists. I saw an opportunity where I could take one of my strengths and use it to create a company, so I started a company that specialized in creating art for games. I then contacted several game publishers and quickly found that my strength fit very well with their needs. It enabled me to create a multi-million dollar company with almost no capital investment.

As you can see in the preceding example, I used one of my strengths—understanding game art production—to build a company. As it turned out, my strength filled a very important role in the industry and allowed me to create partnerships with several larger companies.

Understanding Your Strengths

Before you can understand the strengths of another company, it is important that you take the time to really understand your own company. If your business is even a little successful, you obviously do some things right. Make a list of the things your company does right. It doesn't need to be a long list. In fact, if you can zero in on just one or two main items, it might be better. The idea here is to be able to tell a potential partner in very clear and concise terms why your company is different and better than any of your competitors.

A company strength is something that gives your company an advantage over your competition. For example, maybe your company creates finely machined metal parts for use in building valves. Over the years your team has developed a system for ensuring quality down to the smallest micron.

Because of this system, you are able to offer your clients precision parts that your competitors can't match. Your quality assurance system gives you an advantage over your competition and is a key strength that illustrates why your company is better.

Maybe your company strength is not that you have better quality, but that your manufacturing systems can produce comparable quality for a lot less time and money. Your company strength is that your products are just as good but cost less than your competitors.

Whatever your company strengths are, put them down on paper so that you can see them and express them clearly. Make a short list of the most important ones that pertain to the possible partnership. You will be using these to help you understand how your company can fit with your potential partner.

Understanding Their Strengths

The other part of the strengths equation is to find potential partners whose strengths are in areas that complement your company's strengths. For example, suppose your company has an incredible product but you lack name recognition in the marketplace. As a relatively unknown company, your product is having trouble getting retail shelf space. Your potential partner is a large wholesale distributor with strong ties to many major retailers. They also have a great marketing group who helps their suppliers buy advertising in bulk. Their strengths are compatible with your strength and can certainly help to solve one of your major problems.

Finding the strengths of other companies requires a lot of research. We will go into more depth on how you can understand your potential partners better in Chapter 4. Researching your potential partners is probably one of the most important things you can do before entering into any agreement.

A potential partner's strengths do not always have to match one of your company's weaknesses. Many times two companies with the same strengths make great partners because they share a similar vision. For example, a company with great customer service is more likely to be a good partner with another company that shares that priority than one that does not. Maybe your strength is in innovation; your company prides itself in taking ordinary products and making them extraordinary. You are more likely to find a good partner in a company that strives for the same goal because they will be familiar with the costs of innovation.

Compatible Objectives

Compatible objectives means that the goals of both companies work well with each other and support a symbiotic relationship. In other words, both companies are working toward goals that complement each other.

Several years ago I had a partnership with a larger company in which we were writing new software for a very competitive market. Our partner needed to have some very innovative features to gain market share on their competition. Because our company was still very young, we needed greater name recognition in the larger marketplace. At the beginning of the project we mapped out a plan that brought new functionality to the product that was truly unique and innovative. It was something that hadn't been seen in the market before.

Because we were trying to do something new, the development process was longer and more expensive than other projects of the same type we had done before. We had to invest significant resources to the task and there were many times during the course of development that both companies questioned whether it would be worth the effort.

In the end we were both rewarded because not only did we achieve our goal of bringing something innovative to the market, our notoriety in the industry skyrocketed. It gave both companies a boost going forward.

Company Objectives

An *objective* deals with forward strategy. It is part goal, part wish, and part purpose of a company's existence. Some companies simply have a goal to earn money. Other companies may have some altruistic purpose such as relieving suffering or feeding the homeless. Often companies have multiple objectives. Sometimes one company objective may be at odds with other company objectives. For example, I was involved with a company that had a stated objective of being at the leading edge of new technology. They also had an objective of paying premium wages to all their employees. These two objectives often were in conflict with each other. In order to remain on the leading edge of technology the company had to invest tremendous resources in research and development. These investments reduced the company profits, making it difficult to pay the premium wages they wanted to their employees. In order to keep cash-flow within the company sound they found themselves having to work on products that were not innovative or cutting edge. This caused friction and conflict among the employees because the reason they came to the company was because they wanted to work on leading edge technology.

Like company strengths, you also need to have a clear picture of your company objectives. What does your company want to be when it grows up? Does your company have a purpose? Are all of your company's objectives compatible with each other? Before you talk with a potential partner you should answer the preceding questions as honestly and completely as you can.

Often a company objective is not a current strength of the company because objectives are future goals. It is something the company is working toward in hopes that it will one day be a strength. Very early on, Microsoft established a company objective of every home having a computer running Microsoft software. At the time they made that a company objective, computers were only in a very small percentage of homes, however, the objective gave the company a way to measure their success and a direction for making company decisions. It is arguable that Microsoft's dominance in the computer market can be attributed to their company objective.

Having an objective turns a company's attention to the future and what can happen rather than just looking at the present and what has happened. Where a company is headed is more important than where a company is today when it comes to making good partnerships. If your objective is to double in size in the next two years and your partner is only interested in maintaining market share against aggressive competition, you will likely find that there will be a conflict in philosophy between the two companies. If, on the other hand, your partner also wants to be aggressive and grow their market segment, then there is a better likelihood that the partnership will work.

Don't be afraid to ask about company objectives when meeting with a potential partner. A company's objectives are a legitimate concern for any two companies contemplating a partnership. Don't just take a company objective at face value, however. Compare the company objective with what the company is actually doing and where it is headed in the marketplace. Just because a company has a stated objective doesn't mean that it is going to achieve that objective. Follow your initial questions with other questions that drill deeper into the matter.

As an example, suppose your potential partner has a company objective of being a leader in the personal health market. If the company mainly creates "me too" products that are duplicates of branded competitive products, then they are not likely to reach their goal. If, on the other hand, they are consistently introducing new, innovative products of their own that others want to copy, then there is a better chance that they will reach their goal. Follow questions about what company objectives are with questions about how the company is reaching those objectives. See if they are willing to show a history of improvement toward their objective. Most importantly, determine whether your partnership with them is directly related to their company objective. A discussion of company objectives is one of the easiest ways to gain valuable information about your potential partner.

Fair to Both Parties

For any partnership to be successful it has to be fair to both parties. Too often a partnership will favor one partner's interests over the other. These types of partnerships tend to have a high failure rate, and if they do succeed, they don't last very long. If a partner company—in its zeal to protect its own interests—pushes for an agreement that unfairly restricts or hinders its partner in any way, there is bound to be resentment. A good partnership between two companies should be fair to both partners.

In the entertainment business, for example, large movie studios routinely demanded all the ancillary rights from the creators of the property. If an author wanted to turn a story into a movie, typically the author had to give the movie studio all the rights to all ancillary incarnations of the property. This meant the movie studio could then sell the video game rights or TV rights to the story. They also controlled any merchandising rights for putting the characters from the story on coffee mugs or t-shirts.

The movie studios argued that they deserved these ancillary rights because the popularity of the story was going to be based in large part on the popularity of the movie. However, the authors and screen writers who created the stories were not happy because not only did they seldom see any revenue from ancillary rights, they also gave up all control to the movie studios. As other media like video games and television gained in popularity, licensing fees for these rights increased and became a significant revenue source for the studios, but it generally didn't trickle down to the original author.

Frustrated with the amount of control given to the movie studios, authors began to look for other potential partners to create movies of their work. This led to a proliferation of independent production companies that were more willing to let the authors retain control of some ancillary rights. These production companies, while not as large or powerful as the major studios, soon started gaining ground in the industry as some of them started making deals for major properties. Today, the motion picture industry is very different than what it was in years past. While resentment of the major studios is only a part of the reason for these firms existence, the fact that production deals seemed unfair played a major role in their development.

For a partnership to be successful over a long period of time there has to be a willingness on the part of both partners to be fair. Long term relationships require all parties in those relationships to be aware of the needs of their partners.

Being fair doesn't mean being equal, though. It isn't fair for one partner to take the majority of the risk while both partners share equally in the rewards. It also isn't fair for one partner to do all the work while both partners share equally in the rewards. If a partnership is a 50/50 partnership, both parties need to bring equal amounts of capital and effort to the partnership, otherwise one or the other partner will be resentful. The size of the company doesn't always dictate the partnership percentage. In many joint ventures between companies the larger company is the minority stakeholder supplying capital while the smaller company does all the work. Every situation is different and should be looked at independently to ensure that it is fair.

Before entering into a partnership with another company, you should take the time to clearly define what each partner will bring to the relationship. Put everything out on the table so that both partners can see the value of what the other partner is contributing. After there is an agreement on contributions, it is often easier to agree on rewards. If the relationship is to be a long one, it is a good idea to meet again every year or so and go through the process again. If one or the other partner feels something is unfair, it can usually be worked out in these annual meetings before the problem becomes too big to solve.

I have had a couple of partnerships that didn't work out, and in both cases the problem seemed to boil down to one or more of the partners feeling that other members of the partnership were unfairly gaining more than they deserved for the work or capital they brought to the partnership. This feeling of unfairness was a minor annoyance in the beginning of the partnership but over time it grew to the point that there simply was no way to fix it. If there are any feelings of unfairness, all members of the partnership need to deal with them while they are still on good terms with each other and before minor resentments become major problems.

Both Are Trustworthy

Trust is vital to a good working partnership. Being able to trust your partner to hold up their part of an agreement is the foundation of a good working relationship because both parties can then focus on building the business without having to second guess their partner. A partnership without trust will usually cause undue stress on a partnership because both parties will always be looking for the other partner to do something to undermine the partnership.

In the spectrum of trust there are two extremes: total blind trust and paranoia. Neither is good for a healthy partnership. Total blind trust will almost always lead to disaster because it is too easy for one partner to take advantage of the other. Paranoia, on the other hand, is even worse because it brings fear into the relationship, causing the partners to spend more time checking up on each other than getting actual work done. In business there must be safeguards put in place that give partners reason to trust each other.

Trust is something that we earn and it should not be given lightly. To really trust someone generally means that we have tested that trust over a long period of time in multiple circumstances. Unfortunately, most new partnerships are created between two parties that have relatively little experience with each other. On the one hand, for the partnership to work there has to be trust between the two companies. On the other hand, the two companies are new to each other and likely have no direct evidence of the other party's trustworthiness. To overcome this dilemma, partnerships usually will create a partnership agreement.

Partnership Agreement

A *partnership agreement* is a legal contract between the two companies forming the partnership that clearly lays out each partner's responsibilities and sets forth rewards for compliance and penalties for noncompliance. A good partnership agreement will be very clear and detailed in how the partnership is supposed to work and the role of each partner in that partnership.

Having a detailed partnership agreement does not mean that you distrust your partner. In fact the agreement should be just the opposite. It should be the foundation upon which trust will be built. The agreement helps to establish the expected trust that will develop between the two companies over the course of the partnership.

In the "Agreement Clearly Laid Out and Well Understood by Both Parties" section later in this chapter, we will go into more detail about what should be contained in a partnership agreement.

Trust Begins with You

Before concerning yourself with how trustworthy your partner might be, you should first make sure your company is worthy of a partner's trust. Do you honor your agreements, even the little ones? When checking out a potential partner, larger companies will routinely contact other companies that have done business with their potential partner. Depending on how important the partnership is to them they may contact vendors who sell to your company or even former employees of your company. They want references for how you conduct your business, and they want to know how you treat your obligations and responsibilities.

Not only is it reasonable for them to do a background check on your company, in some industries it is expected. You shouldn't look at their investigation of your company as an intrusion on your privacy or paranoia on their part. You should welcome the opportunity because it is a way for them to vicariously develop trust in you and your company. If you have always done your best to make sure your company lives up to every commitment it makes no matter how small, they are likely to uncover just that and the impression will be quite favorable. Given the choice between dealing with two potential partners, a larger company will almost always go with the company that is perceived to be the more honest, even if they are more costly.

There are very few companies that have a spotless record. Often through no fault of your own, you may have a disagreement with a former employee or have a problem with a vendor or client. It happens even to the best companies. To help potential partners contact people that you trust to give you a good recommendation, compile a list of references that you can provide to your potential partner. This will do two things: One, it will let them know that you understand they need to check you out and that you encourage it. Two, it will ensure that they have references that will be positive toward your company.

Before you hand a reference list to any potential partner, you should speak to each reference and ask them if they will be a reference for you. This will give you a chance to find out if they are willing to endorse your company and also let them know that they may be contacted.

Trusting Your Partner

Okay, so you trust yourself and your company, do you trust your partner? Earlier I stated that trust is earned, not just given. If you have limited working experience with your potential partner, though, you must use other means to determine whether you can trust your partner. When dealing with a large organization there are a number of ways that you can check to see how your potential partner has performed in the past. Because large companies are usually public companies with significant public exposure, it is often easier for you to find information about them than it is for them to find information about you.

Ask Your Peers

If you don't have direct experience with a company, borrow it from someone else. In most industries there are many opportunities to meet and talk with companies that are similar to yours. These companies represent a significant resource for comparing notes about larger companies they have experience with. Usually you can gather valuable information about companies you intend to do business with. The best part about this information is that you are talking to people who have real experience with your target company and can tell you a lot about their experience.

Ask for References

Don't be afraid to ask your potential partner for references. They will likely give you only favorable references, but those references are just as important as any others because they can indicate how a good relationship can work with the company. Not only are you looking for trustworthiness, you are also looking to find best practices for working relationships with that company.

Public Documents

One of the best ways to learn something about your potential partner is to read their annual report. In it you will find a wealth of important information that will help to give you a feel for the company. Public companies are required by law to disclose to the public significant information about the company, and one of the items they must report is any and all legal proceedings brought against the company. Look carefully through the proceedings for instances where there were problems with past partners. You can often contact the company that brought the lawsuit; they may give you important information about the company that you may not find anywhere else.

Former Employees

There are a number of places where you can find former employees of a company. One good resource on the Web is www.linkedin.com, where you can search for current and former employees of a company. You can also send them a message asking for a reference for that company.

Companies within a Company

One final important note to make about trust and large companies is that because of their size there can be vast differences between one part of a large company and another. Some companies are so large that their individual divisions are themselves large companies. Within major divisions there can also be a number of working groups, and each group may have its own process for dealing with smaller partners. Any research you do regarding the trustworthiness of a company should be directed not only to the company in general but more specifically to the part of the company that you will be dealing with directly.

Agreement Clearly Laid Out and Well Understood by Both Parties

The partnership agreement will form the foundation of your relationship with your partner company. If done right, it will contain the details that will protect you and your company's interests that may not have been part of the verbal negotiation. Its purpose is to set forth how the two companies will work with each other and what the rewards for the partnership will be for each partner. It will also define what happens if there is a breakdown in the partnership and how that breakdown will be handled.

While no agreement can anticipate every eventuality, it should contain a number of elements to ensure a clear understanding on both sides of how things are intended to work.

> **NOTE**
>
> We are not attorneys and are not qualified to give you legal advice. As with any legal issue, you should consult a qualified attorney. Our observations are based on our own business experiences and are coming from the viewpoint of a business owner.

- Full legal names of companies and contact information
- Description of the relationship
- Obligations and benefits of each party
- Ownership rights
- Confidentiality
- Dissolution
- Warranties and indemnities
- Signatures

Legal Names and Contact Information

The beginning of a contract should clearly state the legal names of the companies involved in the contract. It should also contain information about the type of company and in what state each company involved in the contract is registered. It is also a good idea to put down a contact person and a contact address for any official communications regarding the contract. Having this information at the beginning of the contract is helpful in case there is a need to send official correspondence.

Description of Relationship

It is very important for both parties to understand what their relationship will be and how it will function. This includes the structure of the partnership and the authority each partner has to make decisions for the partnership, as well as any methods or procedures either party needs to go through to complete their obligations for the partnership. Sometimes the relationship will be described in detail in a specific section of the contract but most of the time it will involve several sections. As a business owner you need to read the agreement carefully and make note of all relationship issues.

Structure

The structure of your relationship is what will serve as the vehicle through which your partnership will move forward. Often it is just a contractual agreement between two parties, however, sometimes it may be that a separate business entity is created, such as in the case of a joint venture. Each type of structural set up will have its own set of criteria and obligations. Some will take more effort to administer than others, including handling details like tax liabilities and registration with the state. Consult with your attorney and accountant to make sure you are familiar with how the structure of the relationship will affect your company.

There are a number of ways to structure a partnership. The most common is a *work for hire* relationship in which one partner hires the other for a specific job. In a work for hire relationship there is a contracting party and a contractor; the contractor performs a service and the contracting party pays for that service.

Another type of structure for a partnership is a modification of the work for hire agreement in which the contractor is entitled to a portion of the proceeds from the work. These types of agreements are often called *royalty agreements;* they are common in the publishing, entertainment, and software industries but can also be found in just about any industry. In these agreements the contracting party's payment is in the form of an advance against a royalty percentage. When the product goes to market, the advance is recouped first and then anything beyond the advance is paid to the contractor.

Sometimes partnerships are based on a licensing agreement. In this case one party wants to use a property owned by the other party to enhance their product. For example, suppose a clothing maker wants to manufacture a line of clothing based on a popular children's movie character. The clothing manufacturer pays the movie company a licensing fee that often includes a royalty in exchange for an agreement that the clothing company can use images and other intellectual property for their clothing line.

A more equal partnership may include a joint venture. In a *joint venture* (JV) the two companies come together to form a third company that is owned by the two companies jointly. The joint venture is a legal business entity on its own; it pays its own taxes and is responsible for its own expenses. Ownership of the JV is usually dependent on the investment of each partner.

Another type of partnership is a *merger* or *acquisition*. In this case one of the partners simply buys the other partner. In a merger the two companies come together to form a single company. In an acquisition, the acquiring company buys the other company and absorbs it into itself.

Regardless of how your partnership is structured, it is critical that you understand the ramifications it will have on your current company and how it will affect it going forward.

Obligations and Benefits of Each Party

Contracts will layout specific obligations and benefits for each party. That is what a contract is for: to detail what benefits each party derives from the partnership and also to define what each party has to do to gain those benefits.

As you read through a contract, it is very important that you take special note of any language that defines what your company receives. It may be as simple as just receiving payment for services, but there are many other types of benefits that it may also include. Some partnerships will give your company access to technology, facilities, know-how, marketing resources, production, warehousing, intellectual property, health care, funding sources, and any number of other benefits. If there are specific benefits you want in the partnership and they are not outlined in the contract, you should bring them up as part of the contract negotiation. It is always better to have it in writing.

Obligations are as important if not more important for you to make note of in a contract. It doesn't matter what is said in negotiation, what is written in the contract is what you are obligating yourself and your company too. Obligations can range from paying certain funds to doing certain work. They may also include specific procedures that your company must follow. The more clearly defined your obligations are the more likely your company will be to fulfill them. Make sure you understand each one.

Ownership Rights

Ownership rights are the rights given to each company in the contract. These rights include intellectual property rights such as copyrights, trademarks, and patents, but they may also include actual physical property as well. You need to understand both what rights you will be giving up and what rights you will be gaining. (In Chapter 3 we will cover protecting what you own in greater detail.)

Confidentiality

Contracts usually will define what business information needs to be kept confidential and what is public, and the information is usually found in a section labeled Confidentiality. Confidentiality protects both you and your partner. Pay special attention to the confidentiality section to ensure that your company is protected and that you understand what obligations you will be under with regard to the confidential information of your partner.

Almost all contracts are considered proprietary information and, therefore, are considered confidential information.

Dissolution

At some point the partnership will end, and many times the end of the partnership will be spelled out in the contract. For example, a contract may be for a specific time with an option to renew or it may be for a specific task such as the completion of a project or the development of a product. In these instances the contract will indicate when the partnership will end and how it will be completed.

Options to renew or continue the partnership usually involve an option to renew or extend the contract under specific conditions that have to be met by both parties. Another option to renew may be a First Right of Refusal clause, which gives one or the other party the right to be presented a new deal and refuse or accept it before it is shown to third parties.

Almost all contracts will have surviving obligations that last beyond the completion of the contract. These obligations include things like confidentiality and maintenance.

There may also be termination rights in the contract for one or both parties. These rights are there to help dissolve the partnership in certain situations when the partnership is causing a problem for one or the other party.

Warranties and Indemnities

Warranties are legal representations that the contracting parties make to each other. They generally include things such as ownership of certain property or the assurance that certain key personnel will be involved in the execution of the work. Make note of any warranties you make in a contract as they carry legal obligations.

Indemnities are legal situations in which one party guarantees that the other party will not be held responsible. For example, one party may wish to be indemnified against any work-related accidents. The important thing here is to understand what indemnities are granted and how they work. Warranties and indemnities are good items to go over with your attorney to make sure you understand what they entail.

Signatures

This may seem a little obvious but it is still important: Contracts are valid based on the signatures of those who are responsible. If you are signing your name to a document, you know you need to be careful about what is in the document. It is also important to make sure that you have the authority to sign the document. This may mean you need to get approval from the board of directors or other stake-holders in the company. In some cases contracts can be held as invalid if the signing party did not get the proper approval to sign it.

Just as it is important for you to have the authority to sign the contract, it is also important that you know that the person signing the contract for your partner company also has that authority. It is reasonable for you to ask that question in the course of the contract negotiation.

In this section we have covered just a few of the important aspects of a partnership agreement. There are many more aspects that your attorney may feel are also important. We cannot stress enough the importance of having adequate specialized legal counsel in all aspects of partnership and contract negotiation.

Clear Mechanism for Ending Partnership

Not every partnership will work as intended. There are many reasons why a partnership can go bad. Maybe the staff in your partner's company has changed. Maybe the market conditions have changed. Maybe there has been a breach in the agreement and the partnership needs to end. If something happens to make the partnership unworkable, how can you gracefully disentangle your company from the partnership?

Although you may never need to end a partnership, you should be prepared to do so just in case. There should be an understanding between you and your partner of how the partnership should end if it has to. You need to know under what circumstances you or your partner can terminate the agreement.

Termination of a partnership is almost always unpleasant, but it doesn't have to be adversarial. If both parties craft an agreement that deals with the separation in a fair and equitable manner, the process can be achieved with minimal damage to both parties.

For termination to be fair, it has to balance the need to persevere through challenges with the reality of an unworkable situation. If termination is too easy and lacks clear criteria for why termination is necessary, the partnership may never get a chance to reach its full potential because of a few difficult problems. On the other hand, if termination is too difficult and the criteria so stringent that termination is nearly impossible, both parties could be in a detrimental position for a long time.

In most partnership agreements, there are two types of termination clauses: termination for cause and termination without cause. *Termination for cause* means that one party materially breached the partnership agreement and made the partnership unworkable. *Termination without cause* means that something outside the partnership, like market conditions or government regulations, has changed and the partnership is no longer practical. Each of these types of termination needs to be handled differently.

Termination for Cause

It is almost always better to try to work out problems in a partnership agreement between the two parties than it is to invoke a termination clause. Usually there is a logical explanation for an unforeseen problem by the offending party and with a little understanding and patience the problem might well be resolved and the partnership saved. In any situation where there is a material breach of an agreement, there should be a *cure period* that gives the breaching party enough time fix the problem. Only if there is no willingness on the breaching party's part to fix the problem does it make sense to end the relationship.

Cure periods should be long enough to give the breaching party time to fix the problem but not so long that it destroys either company's ability to operate. In most cases it is 30 days, but in some cases it may need to be shorter or longer depending on the type of partnership. For example, suppose there is a clause in the agreement that a specific person is critical to the work—a licensing agreement with a celebrity may have such a clause. If the celebrity becomes injured or ill, it may mean that there is an inability for that particular person to fulfill obligations in the agreement. This could technically be a breach of the agreement. However, if there is sufficient time the celebrity may recover or find a substitute for the obligations of the agreement. Rather than terminating the agreement, there could be multiple solutions that will still provide adequate representation while the celebrity recovers.

If, however, even after a sufficient cure period there are still significant problems with the performance of the breaching party, the agreement may need to be terminated. Usually termination for breach includes strong penalties for the breaching party. The penalties serve two purposes: They help to heal the damage the breaching party created for the non-breaching company, and they also provide strong incentive for both parties to live up to their side of the agreement. If there is no penalty for breaching an agreement, the agreement is too weak.

Penalties for breach may include a refund of money, return of intellectual property, injunctions against exploitation of a product, or any number of other remedies that help to heal the non-breaching party. When considering a termination for cause clause in a contract, you should take a look at what damage could be sustained should your partner breach the contract and then incorporate penalties that protect your company's interests. If you make the penalties unreasonable or excessively punitive, however, you run the risk of them not standing up in court or reluctance on your partner's side to agree to the clause. Remember, too, that it works both ways: Your partner will also want penalties in place in the case that you breach the contract.

There should also be specific criteria outlining exactly what constitutes a material breach of an agreement. Things that are out of a partner's control should not be considered a breach of the agreement. For example, if an agreement is between a retailer and a distributor and a traffic accident or a natural disaster makes it impossible for timely delivery to the retailer, it should not be considered a breach of the agreement as long as the distributor made sufficient effort to deliver the products. On the other hand, if the distributor got a new client and gave them priority over the retailer, thereby causing delays and chronic shortages of goods, then that could be grounds for a breach of the agreement.

The best way to approach a breach of an agreement is to take a close look at the obligations of each partner and then project what might happen if there were non-performance for each obligation. State clearly in your agreement what constitutes breach for each party and what notifications and cure periods are available to that party in the event of a breach of contract.

Termination without Cause

Termination without cause (or *termination for convenience* as it is sometimes called) is a little trickier than termination for cause because there is not a breach of the agreement by either partner. In this situation there isn't so much a problem with a partner as there is a problem with the environment in which the partnership is working. For example, consider the case of a partnership that is in the process of creating a new product that stores data for convenient use with computers and other electronic devices. During development they find that a new technology has changed the way people want to store their data, making the partnership's technology obsolete. Continuing the partnership would not make sense because the market changed.

The example above actually happened. As computer data became larger and more bulky during the mid- to late 1990s, the old standard of magnetic disks became too small to hold enough data to be practical. Several solutions emerged, including larger magnetic drives, CD/DVDs, and even mini-optical disks. Many companies were working in these technologies to update and perfect them for the mass market. During this time, though, a technology known as a USB drive hit the market. USB drives were solid state and had no moving parts. They were relatively inexpensive and very small. They also had massive storage capabilities, exceeding even DVDs in storage capacity while at the same time being universally easy to use for reading and writing new data. USB drives became so popular that they completely changed the market for other storage devices.

Because the USB drive was so popular the demand for disk drives began to dry up. Most of the companies researching disk drive solutions either went out of business or had to change their direction. Contracts had to be modified or terminated to deal with the market change. Some companies opted to close and disband. Others switched their research to other areas. Those that were more flexible survived while those that were too focused on a single solution didn't. There were a lot of tough decisions for everyone involved.

There are many reasons for terminating an agreement without cause, including changes in government regulations, natural disaster, loss of funding, changes in company direction, changes in the economy, and even more attractive opportunities. Whatever the reason, they need to be balanced with the obligations partners have to each other. If one partner relies on the partnership for a significant portion of its business, the termination of the agreement, for whatever reason, could be a major hardship for that company. Therefore, termination without cause should never be a simple decision, but rather one that is thought out thoroughly.

There needs to be a disincentive for a party to terminate the partnership agreement for convenience. This is important because it protects the integrity of the partnership. If one party needs to terminate the agreement because their circumstance has changed, they need to be willing to compensate the other party for the time and effort of replacing the work they would have otherwise gained through the partnership. For example, if I am running a book publishing company and one of my main partners is a printing company that does a substantial amount of printing for my company, there needs to be a clause in our agreement that deals with what happens if I want to change to another printer. The printer gives me a huge discount because of the volume of work my company represents; this is a benefit to me from our arrangement. The benefit to the printer is that they can count on a certain amount of work every month from my company. If I find a source for printing overseas that is more attractive to me than the current deal I have with my current printer, it is only fair that I compensate them for the problems that result from my change in business. Thus, to cancel our agreement I agree to pay the printer a predetermined amount or wait and continue to fulfill our agreement until it expires.

The idea is to make the termination fair without inflicting undue injury to one of the partners. In the example above, my benefit of cheaper printing has to be weighed against the cost of terminating the agreement.

As with termination for cause, it is always better to talk directly to your partner in the event of a market condition change. It is likely that market conditions have changed for them as well and together you may be able to craft a new agreement that maintains the partnership while addressing the change in the market. If the partnership is truly successful, then there should be some ability to roll with the punches and still keep a good partnership intact.

Win/Win: Better to Walk Away Than to Enter a Bad Relationship

A *win/win relationship* is one where both companies are improved through partnering with each other. In other words, good partnerships are derived from recognition that the health and well being of your partner company is just as important to the partnership—and to your own company's success—as the health and well being of your own company. Hardnosed, selfish company tactics may win you a "great deal" in the short term, but it will not build that lasting, trusting relationship that works over the long haul, and it certainly won't give you opportunities to expand and enhance your partnership. Taking a win/win stance in your partnership arrangement will, on the other hand, not only make your partnership work better but it will also give you the ability to work together to take advantage of new and better opportunities as they present themselves.

Win/win relationships in business go well beyond simply being fair with each other. They entail an attitude change in the way issues and problems are approached. The idea is not to simply look at problems and how they will affect your own company, but rather to look at how the problems and issues also affect your partner. It also means that you place as much emphasis on making sure your partner is doing well as you do on your own company. This may mean that you look at things from an ecosystem point of view.

If your company were in the paper manufacturing business, for example, you would likely have partners who are in the lumber business. These partners are your source of raw materials. If enough of them go under because of hard economic times, your source of lumber becomes more and more limited. On the other hand, if they are healthy, vibrant companies that continue to grow and do well, you have a much better opportunity in the future to get all the raw materials you need to continue to make paper.

In a narrow view, one or two of your partners going out of business may not result in problems for your company, but in the long term it can have a net negative effect on your business.

There is another positive side to a good partnership in being able to leverage the know-how and human capital from both companies to take advantage of future opportunities. Usually in the course of a partnership there is a significant amount of growth that takes place. The companies learn to get along with each other and they become accustomed to how they work together. If something innovative is uncovered during the course of the partnership, there is a higher likelihood that the innovation will be shared if the working relationship is vibrant, open, and caring.

If I know that my interests are just as important to you as they are to me, I am more likely to share important information with you. If I also see that our working together has created an environment that fosters progress and innovation, and I know that in working together we have a much better chance of exploiting my ideas, I will have significant incentive to bring my ideas forward and contribute to the growth of the partnership. By adopting a win/win attitude not only between the management but also between everyone else involved in the partnership, you can multiply the possibilities for both companies.

In today's economy no company, especially a small one, can go it alone. You need friends and allies to make it through the land mines and traps. Your closest allies are your partners. If you both look out for each other, together you can conquer any problem and take advantage of any opportunity that comes along. Not every partnership can be a win/win partnership, but finding one that is can make all the difference in the world.

Chapter 3

Protecting Your Company

One reason smaller companies often pass up opportunities to work with larger companies is that the owners are afraid of losing proprietary technology or trade secrets that they feel give their company a competitive advantage. While there will always be unscrupulous business people who will take advantage of smaller companies, the vast majority of larger businesses are very cautious to adhere to a strict definition of property rights because the last thing they want is to have an important product or service interrupted by an infringement lawsuit. There is an old saying that "good fences make good neighbors," which in this case means that clear definitions and strong contracts benefit both parties in a partnership.

While there are legitimate reasons to be cautious when approaching any partnership, there are many tools and methods available to help protect your company's important property. In this chapter we will examine several ways you can protect yourself and your company so that you have confidence in your negotiations with larger companies.

Before we begin we must make one disclaimer: While we are confident in the methods we describe in this chapter, the information related here is not meant to replace the direct consultation of an attorney. Laws differ from state to state and from country to country. Circumstances and situations differ from company to company, and a method that might work well in one industry may not work as well in another. Our discussions in this chapter are meant to give broad guidelines, not specific advice. When approaching any potential partnership with a larger company it is always a good practice to have a qualified attorney review your property protection measures and give you specific advice for each circumstance.

The methods and measures you take as a business owner to protect your company's proprietary property will vary greatly depending on the type of property you want to protect. For example, a specific invention might be protected by a patent, while specific lines of software code might be protected with a copyright. Property such as a software product might be protected by a number of different methods, but other trade secrets may have no direct legal protection other than just keeping them secret. To simplify the information in this chapter, we will first examine a method of property protection and then discuss which types of proprietary property are best protected using this method. The methods we will examine in this chapter are as follows:

- Nondisclosure agreements
- Patents
- Copyrights
- Trademarks and service marks
- Trade secrets
- Contracts

Nondisclosure Agreements

In many industries it is a common practice to enter into a nondisclosure agreement prior to discussing any substantive partnership issues. A *nondisclosure agreement* (or NDA) is an agreement between two parties to keep confidential any information disclosed by either party. The idea is to protect proprietary or sensitive information from becoming public. It is also a means of ensuring that anything owned by one party or the other remains the property of its respective owner.

Good nondisclosure agreements will have clear language regarding what information will be kept confidential and what will not. They will contain clear penalties and remedies in the event confidential information is disclosed to a third party. To help you understand what a nondisclosure agreement looks like, consider the example featured on the following pages.

This example is a good basic nondisclosure agreement; it is good for most business purposes. It doesn't, however, deal with specific situations or industries. If you have specific information that you feel is vitally important to your company, you may want to mention specifically in the agreement what that information is so that there will be no mistaking its importance.

When negotiating a partnership, the purpose of the nondisclosure agreement is to allow both parties to discuss all aspects of their business freely without the worry of either party taking advantage of those discussions. It is almost impossible for any business relationship to progress toward a formal partnership without the ability to speak freely, and a good nondisclosure agreement helps to enable open discussions while protecting the parties involved at the same time.

Most large companies are willing to sign a nondisclosure agreement, in fact they will often ask you to sign one before you bring it up yourself. Large companies generally have their own agreement that they will want you to sign. It is usually a better idea, when possible, to sign theirs than it is to try to get them to sign one of yours. This is because any outside agreement will be sent to the company's legal department and it may be weeks before they return it to you. A better, more timely method is to take their agreement and read it carefully. If there is anything in their agreement that you don't understand, seek advice from a qualified intellectual property attorney.

Non-Disclosure Agreement

THIS AGREEMENT (the "Agreement") is made between:

_____ a(n) _____ corporation,

and _____ a(n) _____ corporation,

and entered into this _____ day of _____, _____.

WHEREAS, the Parties possess certain Confidential Information as defined herein, and wish to disclose in confidence to each other such Confidential Information pursuant to the terms of this Agreement in order to allow each Party to evaluate such Confidential Information, and

WHEREAS, each Party wishes to receive such Confidential Information for evaluation purposes only and determine if it desires to enter into a subsequent business relationship with the other Party;

In consideration of the mutual promises and covenants contained in this Agreement, the Parties agree as follows:

Definitions

"Confidential Information" means information that the disclosing Party designates as being confidential or which under the circumstances surrounding disclosure ought to be treated as confidential, including but not limited to disclosure made orally, in writing, via electronic transmission, or fixed in any other tangible medium such as a computer storage device. "Confidential Information" includes, without limitation, information relating to released or unreleased disclosing Party products, executable software and documents related thereto, the actual computer code of released or unreleased disclosing Party products, the marketing or promotion of any disclosing Party product, disclosing Party's business policies or practices, disclosing Party's business plans and projections, disclosing Party's financial information and projections, the terms of any license agreement of any disclosing Party, and information received from others that disclosing Party is obligated to treat as confidential. Confidential Information disclosed to the receiving Party by any disclosing Party subsidiary and/or agents is covered by this Agreement. Confidential Information shall not include any information that (i) is or subsequently becomes publicly available without the receiving Party's breach of any obligation owed the disclosing Party, (ii) was known to the receiving Party prior to the disclosing Party's disclosure of such information to the receiving Party and evidenced in a writing, or (iii) became known to the receiving Party from a source other than the disclosing Party other than by the breach of an obligation of confidentiality owed to the disclosing Party.

Restrictions

The receiving Party shall not use any Confidential Information for any purpose other than an evaluation of whether the receiving Party desires to enter into a subsequent business relationship with the disclosing Party, or disclose any Confidential Information to third parties in any manner without the prior written consent of the disclosing Party. . However, the receiving Party may disclose Confidential Information in accordance with judicial or other governmental order, provided the receiving Party shall give the disclosing Party reasonable notice prior to such disclosure and shall comply with any applicable protective order or equivalent.

The receiving Party shall take all security precautions, at least as great as the precautions it takes to protect its own confidential information, to keep confidential the Confidential Information. The receiving Party may disclose Confidential Information only to the receiving Party's employees or consultants on a need-to-know basis and only for the business evaluation purposes as set forth herein. The receiving Party will have executed or shall execute appropriate written agreements with its employees and consultants sufficient to enable it to comply with all the provisions of this Agreement.

Confidential Information may be used, disclosed, reproduced, summarized or distributed only in pursuance of the receiving Party's business relationship with the disclosing Party, and only as otherwise provided hereunder. The receiving Party agrees to segregate all such Confidential Information from the confidential information and materials of others in order to prevent commingling.

The receiving Party may not reverse engineer, decompile or disassemble any software disclosed to the receiving Party.

Rights and Remedies

The receiving Party shall notify the disclosing Party immediately upon discovery of any unauthorized use or disclosure of Confidential Information, or any other breach of this Agreement by the receiving Party, and will cooperate with the disclosing Party in every reasonable way to help the disclosing Party regain possession of the Confidential Information and prevent its further unauthorized use.

The receiving Party shall return all originals, copies, reproductions and summaries of Confidential Information at the disclosing Party's request, or, at the disclosing Party's option, certify destruction of the same.

The receiving Party acknowledges that monetary damages may not be a sufficient remedy for unauthorized disclosure of Confidential Information and that the disclosing Party shall be entitled, without waiving any other rights or remedies, to such injunctive or equitable relief as may be deemed proper by a court of competent jurisdiction.

The disclosing Party may visit the receiving Party's premises, with reasonable prior notice and during normal business hours, to review the receiving Party's compliance with the terms of this Agreement.

Securities Laws

If the disclosing Party is a publicly-held company, the receiving Party understands that the disclosing Party's Confidential Information may be considered material non-public information under Federal and state securities laws and the receiving Party could be found in violation of such laws if the receiving Party takes advantage of such information by (i) trading in the disclosing Party's or any other entity's stock, or (ii) furnishing information to others in connection with the trading of such stock.

Miscellaneous

All Confidential Information is and shall remain the property of the disclosing Party. By disclosing information to the receiving Party, the disclosing Party does not grant any express or implied right to the receiving Party to or under any of the disclosing Party patents, copyrights, trademarks, or trade secret information.

If either Party to this Agreement provides pre-release software as Confidential Information under this Agreement, such pre-release software is provided "as is" without warranty of any kind. The receiving Party agrees that neither the disclosing Party nor its suppliers shall be liable for any damages whatsoever relating to the receiving Party's use of such pre-release software.

This Agreement constitutes the entire agreement between the Parties with respect to the subject matter hereof. It shall not be modified except by a written agreement dated subsequent to the date of this Agreement and signed by both Parties. None of the provisions of this Agreement shall be deemed to have been waived by any act or acquiescence on the part of the disclosing Party, its agent, or employees, but only by an instrument in writing signed by an authorized officer of the disclosing Party. No waiver of any provision of this Agreement shall constitute a waiver of any other provision(s) or of the same provisions on another occasion.

This Agreement shall be construed and controlled by the laws of the State of Utah, and both Parties further consent to jurisdiction by the state and federal courts sitting in the State of Utah. Process may be served on either Party by U.S. Mail, postage prepaid, certified or registered, return receipt requested, or by such other method as is authorized by Utah law.

Subject to the limitations set forth in this Agreement, this Agreement will inure to the benefit of and be binding upon the Parties, their successors and assigns.

If any provisions of this Agreement shall be held by a court of competent jurisdiction to be illegal, invalid or unenforceable, the remaining provisions shall remain in full force and effect.

All obligations created by this Agreement shall survive change or termination of the Parties' business relationship.

IN WITNESS WHEREOF, THE PARTIES HAVE EXECUTED THIS AGREEMENT.

_____   _____

By: _____   By: _____

Name:_____   Name: _____

Title:_____   Title: _____

If you feel that there are problems with a nondisclosure agreement offered to you by the company you wish to partner with, indicate what problems you have with the agreement and any suggested changes you want to see. Remember that any changes to the agreement will have to go through a legal review, but the review will likely be quicker than if you ask them to sign your agreement. You may or may not get all the changes you want in the agreement. If you still have problems with the agreement and the company is unwilling to make the needed changes, you may have to walk away from the potential partnership.

Remember that any agreement between two parties is only as good as either party's word. Just because you have an agreement doesn't mean that the agreement will be honored. One thing that is very important to remember with any potential partnership is that you have to trust your partner. Before you sign any agreement, try to get a feel for the integrity of the company. Take the time to speak with current and former partners—they will be the best source of information about the company and its integrity.

Patents

Patents are a powerful tool for protecting your property. They are granted by the United States Patent and Trademark Office (USPTO), and they give the patent holder the right to exclude others from making, using, offering for sale, selling, or importing their invention. Patents usually last for 20 years, although in some cases one may be able to get an extension.

Patents are primarily designed to protect inventions, but they can also be used to protect methods or systems. An invention is usually a physical object that can be seen, held, or touched but it doesn't have to be. Some inventions are software that only exists as computer code. As technology has advanced the patent office has had to adjust patents to fit new definitions of an invention. Patents also cover methods or systems of doing something. For example, a company may have a manufacturing system for creating better automobile parts. If their system is truly unique, it might get a patent. If you have questions about what can and can't be patented, consult with a patent attorney. They will be able to deal with your specific situation.

Patents do not protect documents or company logos. They also are not useful if you need to keep something secret. Later in this chapter we will discuss how to protect company property that is not protected by a patent.

A patent can be a valuable asset particularly when negotiating with a potential partner. In fact, if the patent is directly related to the part of your business that your potential partner is interested in for the partnership, it can be a great motivator for them to create the partnership. For example, suppose your company holds a patent for a software tool that greatly reduces the time it takes to analyze the strength of a metal alloy. You could find a number of potential partners, from engineering firms to automobile manufacturers, who would be interested in benefitting from your patented asset; in that case it could be a significant source of leverage in any partnership negotiation.

Patents are enforced by the patent holder. What this means is that law enforcement entities do not actively look for patent infringement—it is up to the patent holder to find possible infringements and enforce the patent. However, because a patent is a legal right, the patent holder can use the U.S. court system to enforce the patent.

A U.S. patent is only good within the United States, U.S. territories, and U.S. possessions—just because you have a U.S. patent does not mean that your property is protected in other countries. To fully protect your property you have to be granted a patent in every country in which you want to do business. These are called *international patents*, and they can be quite costly. Before you apply for a patent in every country around the globe, seek the advice of a patent attorney with international experience. Sometimes selecting a few key countries is sufficient to protect your rights.

There are three types of patents offered by the USPTO:

* Utility patents
* Design patents
* Plant patents

Utility Patents

According to the USPTO, "Utility patents may be granted to anyone who invents or discovers any new and useful process, machine, article of manufacture, or composition of matter, or any new and useful improvement thereof." Utility patents are the most common and widely known type of patent. They protect not only an invention but they can also protect a process. For example, if your company has a specific way of creating a product, you may be able to patent that creation process and bar others from using it.

The specific language of the statute states that any person who "invents or discovers any new and useful process, machine, manufacture, or composition of matter, or any new and useful improvement thereof, may obtain a patent."

Based on this definition, almost anything made by man and the process for making it can be patented. However, there are specific rules and guidelines, so you will need to consult a patent attorney to know whether your product or process can be patented using a utility patent.

An example of a utility patent might be a liquid sole inset for athletic shoes. The company shows the patent office that the new sole is more comfortable to wear than other types of soles sold on the market. It also shows that the liquid sole has a way of pulling heat from the foot making it cooler to wear while the athlete is active. These innovations are unique enough that the company is granted a patent. To create the new liquid soles the company had to develop a new manufacturing process that injected the liquid into a specialized cavity in the sole. This new system of manufacturing the shoe sole was also patented. While this example is totally fictitious, it does give an example of what might qualify for a utility patent.

Design Patents

According to the USPTO, "Design patents may be granted to anyone who invents a new, original, and ornamental design for an article of manufacture." Design patents protect only the appearance of an article; they do not protect its function or features.

Design patents can be useful in some instances where the valuable and unique aspect of a product is its design rather than its function. Consult with a qualified patent attorney to learn whether your design qualifies for a design patent.

An example of a design patent could be a new car model design. The design of the car is truly unique and distinctive so the car manufacturer wants to make sure no other company copies it. The design of the car doesn't really change the car's functionality; therefore, the best way to protect it is to obtain a design patent.

Plant Patents

According to the USPTO, "Plant patents may be granted to anyone who invents or discovers and asexually reproduces any distinct and new variety of plant." (Asexually reproduce means to propagate a plant by means other than seeds, such as grafting or budding.) Plant patents apply specifically to plants, so unless you are in the business of creating new plants it probably doesn't apply to your business.

An example of a plant patent might be a new plant discovered by a botanist that has a unique flower. The botanist seeks and obtains a plant patent. The patent protects the development of the new plant to put into production for floral shops.

When to Get a Patent

Just because you can get a patent doesn't always mean that you *should* get a patent. Patents can be expensive, and not all patents are easy to enforce. When looking at a patent, you should first determine whether you can get a patent on your invention, which may require you consulting with a patent attorney. The patent attorney can not only tell you if a patent is available for your invention, she can also help you to understand if your invention can be patented. Sometimes patents may not be available because there are already products that are too similar to your invention. If there are already products or patents for products similar to your, your attorney should be able to find them. If there aren't any similar to yours, then you need to ask *if* you should get a patent. To best determine whether or not you should get a patent you will likely need to get the advice of your patent attorney. You can also seek the advice of other business owners who have experience with patents. In many areas there are business organizations where you can meet other business owners to talk about business topics such as patents.

There may be instances in which a patent will not be the best form of protection for your company's critical assets. A patent is finally published about a year and a half after it is applied for, and in the interim the application information is available to the public. Patents have to be public so others can see if their ideas are already patented. This means that your competition will have access to your critical assets, giving them the ability to create a "similar yet different" product. Also consider that patents are usually only good for 20 years. While you can renew your patent in some cases, if the asset you want to patent is something that you don't want your competitors to have access to any time in the future, a patent might not be the best idea.

The best way to know if you should obtain a patent for any of your company's important assets is to consult with a qualified professional patent attorney. Check around your local area and determine whether there are any good attorneys that you can consult with. When choosing a law firm to handle your patent, check to see whether they have handled patents similar to the one you want to obtain. A firm that primarily handles technology patents might not be the best choice if your patent is in the bio-medical field. Also, always ask for references of previous clients that you can talk with.

Copyrights

Copyrights are protection given to authors of original written works. Written works include anything that can be transcribed, including books, articles, poems, essays, computer code, songs, and so on. To qualify for copyright protection, the written work must be an original work created by the author. It does not have to be a published work. In fact, any written or recorded work can be copyrighted. Painting and photographs can also be copyrighted.

In the U.S., a copyright is assumed as soon as the author creates the work, and a copyright notice (©) can be attached to the author's work when it is created. In fact, it is a good idea to place a copyright notice on all company documents just to be safe. Note that it doesn't have to be registered to be copyrighted. Registering is important, however, if there ever is a dispute over the copyright. By registering the copyright, you create proof of authorship and date of completion, which are very important in any legal proceeding involving a copyright.

Copyrights are registered with the Copyright Office of the Library of Congress. The cost of registering a copyright runs from $35 to $200 or more. There is an online registration process available at http://www.copyright.gov/eco/.

A copyright protects the actual recorded work and gives the author specific rights including the ability to reproduce the work and sell copies of the work, such as in the case of a book or a music CD. It also gives the author the right to publicly perform the work, such as in the case of a piece of music or even dance choreography.

I do a lot of work with software companies. One of the best ways to protect software is to obtain a copyright for the code. The copyright protects the code from anyone making a direct copy of it. The nice thing about copyrights is that entire programs can be copyrighted, but sometimes it is better to break the code out into specific pieces especially if the particular code is unique.

Protecting Copyrights

A copyright only protects the specific work. For example, a copyright will protect the author of a book from someone else publishing copies of the book without the author's permission, but it will not protect the author from someone writing a similar book as long as it can be shown the similar book does not directly quote the original book. Therefore, to enforce a copyright, the author has to show that the infringer has directly copied his or her work.

Like patents, it is up to the copyright holder to enforce the copyright; law enforcement agencies do not enforce copyrights. It is much easier to enforce a copyright if the work in question is registered with the copyright office. Because registering every written work produced by a company can become inordinately expensive, it is usually a good idea to consult with an attorney and develop a plan for determining what should be registered and what should not. A good rule of thumb is to register those documents that are central to the success of the company or those documents that are likely to be available to the public. For example, important company information on the company website should be copyrighted because it is public, but an inter-office memo may not need to be because it is not for public view. Custom computer code that runs critical company software and makes the company more competitive should be registered because of its importance, but plans for the company picnic may not be as important.

One thing to be aware of when registering a work with the copyright office is that anything you register becomes part of the Library of Congress and is available to the public. Therefore you should not register anything that you want to keep secret.

Why Are Copyrights Important?

Copyrights are important because copyrighted material owned by a company becomes part of the company's assets. For some industries such as book publishers and motion picture firms, their copyrighted assets may be their most important and valuable assets. Almost every company has important assets that should be copyrighted, even if it is just a procedure manual for employees, because the company procedures may very well be the reason why the company is successful.

When looking at a partnership with another company, particularly where there is an exchange of assets like in an investment or merger, all company assets are taken into consideration. The company's copyrighted works are part of that consideration.

Copyrights give you and your company legal rights that you can protect under the law. These rights allow you to stop your competition from copying your documents or other protected assets like computer code or company slogans. They also give you the right to copy and distribute products that contain your copyrighted material. With the increasing importance of information in our world today, copyrights will likely continue to increase in importance for every company.

Trademarks and Service Marks

According to the U.S. Patent and Trademark Office "a trademark is a word, phrase, symbol or design, or a combination of words, phrases, symbols or designs, that identifies and distinguishes the source of the goods of one party from those of others." USPTO defines a service mark as "the same as a trademark, except that it identifies and distinguishes the source of a service rather than a product." Both trademarks and service marks are usually referred to as trademarks because they share many of the same attributes.

Trademarks are generally associated with a product brand or a company logo. If they are registered with the U.S. Patent and Trademark Office, they will be designated with a ® symbol. If they are in the process of being registered or are not registered they can be marked with a ™ symbol. The ™ symbol can be placed on any mark or design that you intend to claim right to and should be used where appropriate with any brand label or logo your company wishes to use.

Trademarks protect many of the brand names that we are familiar with. These easily recognized logos are registered for many companies, from the familiar red and white Coca-Cola symbol to the word Hershey in silver on a brown candy bar wrapper. These logos are ubiquitous in our daily lives, and we come to associate them with the products they represent.

Registering your trademark will give you several important privileges:

- A notice to the public that your company claims ownership of the mark.
- A presumption of ownership and the right to use the mark on or in products or services listed in the registration.
- The ability to use the federal court system to enforce the mark.
- A basis for obtaining trademarks in foreign countries.
- The ability to file the mark with the U.S. Customs Office to block foreign companies from importing goods or services with that mark.

In addition to these privileges there are a number of other advantages to having a registered trademark. The most important advantage is that when other companies try to register their marks, your mark will show up in the database. If their mark is similar to yours, theirs will be rejected.

Having your trademark registered also establishes your mark in time and in the public record. A registered trademark symbol shows your company is serious about protecting its property and is in business for the long haul.

Trade Dress

In addition to trademarks and service marks there is also trade dress. *Trade dress* is a designation given to a product or its packaging that makes it unique to a supplier or company. It is a legal term that refers to the physical appearance of a product. It has no size limitations, and can refer to a small consumer product as well as to a large commercial building. Like trademarks, trade dress can be registered with the trademark office and enjoys many of the same privileges of a trademark or service mark.

Trade dress protects packaging. This means that a new kind of egg carton that protect the eggs yet looks very different from traditional cartons is eligible for trade dress protection.

The idea behind trade dress protection is that the act of copying of a product's packaging can result in confusion among consumers when they purchase one product thinking it is another. Trade dress protects the appearance of a product (such as chewing gum) and it can also protect the appearance of a restaurant chain or store chain.

Trademark Importance

Like patents and copyrights, a trademark can be very important when approaching a potential partner. Usually universally known trademarks are the realm of large companies, however, if a small company can achieve public awareness of its trademark, that mindshare can be a hugely valuable asset to the smaller company.

Large companies know the power of a good brand. Brands like Coke, Levis, Kleenex, and others can reach a point that they become synonymous with the product type. Therefore, instead of getting a soft drink you get a Coke. Instead of buying jeans you buy Levis. Instead of asking for a tissue you ask for a Kleenex.

Developing and maintaining a recognizable and trusted brand is something major corporations spend millions on. They understand that the investment in a brand results in customer loyalty and increased profits. They also know that anytime a brand gains traction in a market, it increases the likelihood of success. Therefore, having a good brand represented by a trademarked symbol or brand name is a tremendously valuable asset.

If you feel like your company or your products have strong customer awareness in your market, you should do what you can now—before you begin partnership negotiations—to protect your company or product's image. Trademarks are the first line of defense for maintaining and protecting an image.

Trade Secrets

In some cases the best way to protect something is to keep it secret. One of the big problems with copyrights and patents is that they are public information. This means that your competitors can see your technology, process, system, or idea and potentially make something similar. With a trade secret, the proprietary information of a company is kept secret, and the company takes reasonable precautions to keep the information secret including the use of nondisclosure agreements and noncompete agreements.

Trade secrets do have legal precedent and they do enjoy some legal protection under the law, however the protection differs from that of patents, copyrights, and trademarks. If a company can demonstrate that an employee or another company that they had a nondisclosure or noncompete agreement with used proprietary information, the company can sue for damages.

The concept behind the laws regarding trade secrets is that companies spend a considerable amount of time, effort, and money to develop systems or products that they then use to their advantage in the marketplace. If the company's competitors were able to access the information, the original company's competitive advantage would be unfairly impaired. Trade secrets are, therefore, thought of as intellectual property of the creator and enjoy some protection rights under the law.

Another well known trade secret is the recipe for Kentucky Fried Chicken. The 11 spices used for their chicken has been a closely guarded secret from the beginning.

Forever

Unlike a patent, a trade secret has indefinite protection that doesn't expire after a few years. For example, Coca-Cola's formula for Coke is not patented, it is held as a trade secret. The company has successfully protected its formula for a significantly longer time than the 20 years of protection it would have received from a patent. In theory, a trade secret has no expiration as long as the company maintains reasonable safeguards to protect its intellectual property. In cases where long term protection of company property is important and possible, keeping it as a trade secret might be the best approach.

Problems

One problem with a trade secret is that if another company develops the same or similar technology independently, there is no protection. The only way to protect a trade secret is to show that the other company or individual had access to proprietary knowledge and used that knowledge in the development of a product. As you can see, legal action to protect a trade secret can sometimes become very complicated and costly.

Another significant difference between trade secret protection and patents, copyrights, or trademarks is that they are usually protected under state laws and not under federal laws. The court systems can be very different from state to state and the specific laws may also be different. While most states have adopted the Uniform Trade Secrets Act not all of them have, thus making protecting trade secrets trickier. Like everything else in this chapter, talk with a qualified intellectual properly attorney for specific guidance in your own situation.

Partnership Issues

One of trade secret's greatest attributes can also be one of its biggest drawbacks when it comes to forming a partnership with a major corporation. Because a trade secret relies on being secret for its protection, trade secrets become difficult to deal with when seeking full disclosure from a potential partner. This is particularly the case when the large corporation is looking to partner with your company specifically because of those trade secrets that give your company a competitive advantage. Many otherwise good partnerships have been stalled or abandoned because one or the other party was unwilling to put the company's trade secrets on the table.

I had dealings with one company that had an idea for a product that they wanted to market; however, they were so paranoid about someone stealing their idea that they wouldn't tell anyone what the idea was. It was very frustrating working with them because no one took them seriously. In the end they never did make any headway with their idea and it just died. One of the companies told me that ideas are cheap; it is the execution of the idea that they are really looking for. If the company had not been so secretive about their idea and looked more for a way to get their idea to work, they might have been able to make a partnership.

The problem is not that the two companies don't see value in the partnership or that the partnership is a bad idea. The problem is that the two parties are unable to have a meaningful negotiation because of withheld information. Usually it is because the smaller company is concerned about revealing trades secrets to the larger company. In some cases partnership discussions are not even initiated because of the lack of disclosure. It is difficult for a major corporation, who may see hundreds of business opportunities, to devote a lot of time and effort to a partnership if they can't understand why or how the partnership will benefit them.

The dilemma the small company often faces when contemplating pursuing a partnership with a major corporation is how to give the potential partner enough information to get them interested in the partnership without giving away vital company secrets. Whenever possible, the best route to take is to determine specifically what can be shown without the risk of revealing too much information. Sometimes a well planned system of feeding information to a potential partner can be an advantage. Look at it as a step-by-step process in which you are feeding enough information to keep the potential partner interested but never revealing too much at any given time.

Step One

Start by defining in a very broad way what benefits your company will bring to the partnership. Usually this is done after you have had sufficient contact with or research of the company that you understand how your partnership will best help your potential partner. Lay out a bullet list of specific benefits. Make the bullet items meaningful, but not so detailed that you risk important company intellectual property. At this stage you want to paint a picture of how the two companies can work together to benefit both companies. At this point you are trying to build interest, and that's all.

Step Two

The next step is the trickiest because if your target partner is interested, they are going to want more specific details. They will want to have experts from their company talk with your experts to see if what you have to offer is real or just empty promises. It is perfectly acceptable for you to ask about a nondisclosure agreement between the two companies at this stage, but don't expect one. What is likely to happen will be one of three things:

- *The target partner may sign an NDA.* The NDA is likely to be their own and not yours, but some companies are willing to sign one you create if it is reasonable. If they supply an NDA, read it carefully and have it reviewed by your own attorney to make sure you understand the protections given to you in the agreement. Because there is likely only going to be one NDA, you need to know if it protects your property sufficiently to keep it designated as trade secrets according to your state's laws. If you are comfortable with the agreement, you can sign it and proceed to reveal more in-depth information.

- *The target partner will ask you to sign a disclosure waiver.* This type of document is designed to protect the potential partner and gives you no protection. It will likely say something about the company having its own ongoing research and that anything you show them might or might not be similar to what they are doing. Therefore, they will not be held accountable if they come out with something similar to what you have.

  A disclosure waiver is a difficult document to deal with because it creates a situation in which you are likely giving up trade secret status for anything you show your potential partner. You need to have the document reviewed by a qualified intellectual property attorney to see what you will actually be giving up before you sign it.

- *The target partner will state that an NDA is premature at this stage of the negotiations and all they are really interested in is seeing if what you have is real or not.* That may or may not be the case. It is likely that getting an NDA signed is a big hassle for them and they would rather see what you have before they go through the trouble.

In the first instance you can have more comfort in showing secret information because there is a legally stated understanding that the information you are disclosing is to remain secret and your potential partner is under legal obligation to keep the information secret. You can go ahead and have your expert talk to their expert, but you should still set limits on how detailed the conversations or demonstrations will be. At this early stage you still want to be careful what you reveal. It is better to talk about what you can do rather than how you do it. For example, suppose your company has a special system for training employees to perform difficult medical procedures. Rather than revealing exactly how your system works, it is probably better to show results and statistics that indicate that the system works. Only disclose specific methods on an individual basis and when understanding it will be important to proving its validity.

The latter two situations listed above are more difficult. For one thing, you don't want to lose your trade secret status. In this situation you should first decide if the risk is worth the effort. If the answer is yes, then you will want to carefully orchestrate what you reveal to your potential partner. Anyone who will have contact with the other company needs to be given specific instruction on what they can and cannot say. This is very important, particularly where technology is concerned. Experts from your company and your target partner's company will likely get into deep technical conversations, and it could be very easy for one of your engineers who is passionate about your technology to get carried away explaining it. Make sure you are very clear about what can be talked about and what cannot.

Again, it is often better to talk about the whats instead of the hows. Whenever specific information is requested, give general overviews but not specific functions. You can dangle the carrot that more information is available after serious negotiations are in place.

Step Three

At this point, the two companies have shared information and there is a general consensus that a partnership between the two companies will be beneficial. Now the real negotiations begin. Before entering into specific partnership negotiations, you should be able to insist on an NDA between the two companies. Some companies may still not be willing to sign it, but most will because they will have their own trade secrets that they want to protect. If a company still refuses to sign an agreement, you will need to make the tough decision whether or not you really want that company as a partner. Consider that this may be an indication of how difficult it will be to work with that partner in the future.

When serious negotiations are underway, it is important that both companies are able to learn as much about each other as possible. You want to know everything you can about the company you intend to partner with and you also should want them to know as much as possible about you. A good partnership cannot exist without both partners being willing to work for a clear understanding of roles, responsibilities, and obligations.

During this stage there should be at least a framework of a contract that the two companies are contemplating. That contract should contain language regarding confidentiality. Even though the contract is still being negotiated, it does show intent and is still important. We will talk more about contracts later in this chapter.

Now is the time to be more open with your company's trade secrets. You may still not want to reveal everything, but you can be more specific about how things work. In some situations there may be field tests to see whether what you have to offer will work for the specific needs of your potential partner. This is a legitimate request by your target partner and should be completed if at all possible. A successful field test can be very important in giving your company a boost in negotiations.

Step Four

Step four is usually the final step, in which a binding and detailed contract is signed by both parties. This contract should have very specific language as to exactly what each company is to keep secret and how confidential information is to be handled by both parties. Before signing any such agreement, have your IP attorney review the contract for any intellectual property issues.

As partners it will likely be just as important to your partner that trade secrets are protected as it is to you because they will want to keep their own competitors from gaining access to the information.

Remember that these four steps may not be the same for every situation. In some cases there may only be a couple of steps, while for others there will be several sub-steps in each of the major steps. Just use these steps as a guide to help you through the process.

Contracts

At some stage in the process of forming a partnership with a major company there will be a contract. That contract will likely contain very specific wording regarding the ownership of intellectual property. Understanding how the contract deals with intellectual property will be very important for your partnership.

A contract is a versatile and effective way to designate how ownership of intellectual property is handled in a partnership. In many ways it is a blank page that allows both parties to define what they want for past, current, and new property. It can define joint ownership. It can define exclusive ownership. Sometimes this flexibility is essential to creating a good and workable partnership, particularly in cases where one or the other parties want a method of governing property that is unique or progressive.

A novel approach to ownership of intellectual property is the example of a small production company that created a product that included a set of personalities that were depicted as cartoon characters. The production company had an opportunity to exploit their characters in a video but they didn't want to do the deal with the marketing company if they had to give up the rights to the characters. The marketing company, on the other hand, needed to have the right to sell the videos. To solve the problem the two parties designed a contract in which the marketing company had exclusive right to market and promote the videos without other competing products with the same characters for a period of three years. The production company retained the rights to their characters and the marketing company was able to exploit the video as if they owned the property for a specified period of time. The contract designated how the whole process worked.

Because contracts are so flexible, they are also sometimes very complex and can be hard to understand without the help of a good attorney. Usually a partnership contract will contain much more than just the ownership of intellectual property. They also define working relationships, deliverables, and many other aspects of the partnership relationship.

When dealing with a contract, I find that it is a good idea to create a bullet list of what I think the deal is about and how it should work. I create this list separate from the contract and then compare it to the contract. Sometimes, because contracts have specific legal terms that are hard to understand, I will give the list to an attorney that I trust and who I know will have an opinion. Sometimes there are a few things that aren't quite the way I envisioned them, but more often than not there are a number of issues that I just didn't think about that are additional items that I should have considered.

When dealing with intellectual property issues in a contract, retaining a good attorney to review the contract and highlight any questionable clause is essential. It is always a good idea to have multiple people review the contracts. Some of the important issues that you should look at in the contract are as follows:

- Confidentiality—What are the specific rules that govern who knows what?
- Ownership—Who owns current IP and how will ownership of new IP be designated?
- Protection—How will new IP be protected and who will be responsible for protecting it?
- Exit—How will property be divided when the partnership is over?

Confidentiality

The confidentiality section of the contract will be devoted to defining how proprietary information will be handled between the two companies. In many ways it will look similar to the confidentiality clauses found in an NDA, however, there may be some elements that are specific to the two companies, their industry, and the type of information that is protected. Usually the contract will contain more specific language than an NDA.

Ownership

The ownership section of the contract will be devoted to designating in clear terms the ownership of any current property and how ownership will be divided for any new property developed jointly by the partners.

Protection

Property protection is sometimes included in ownership clauses and sometimes it is separate. It should specify a clear and understandable way to deal with property protection and state who is responsible for obtaining that protection, whether it be patent, trademark, or another form of protection.

Exit

Detailing an exit strategy in the contract will save time and misunderstandings later. It is better to deal with the issues in the beginning and not make any assumptions. If you have important intellectual property, make sure the contract deals with it specifically and fully. No business partnership lasts forever. Some may last generations, but there will always be an end of an adjustment to the deal. It is better to anticipate a breakup of the partnership and specify how things will be handled than to be surprised when things don't go your way.

Property Protection and Your Business

Protecting a company's property is very important, but there will be times when it can stall or slow down the partnership process. In the course of negotiating with a larger company, it can feel like you are exposing too much information. Often tough decisions of trust and integrity have to be made without complete or even adequate protection. As the business owner, your best course of action is to evaluate the risks and rewards of any business deal and weigh them as best you can with the information you have. To help guide you in these decisions, here are some helpful suggestions:

- Companies that routinely take advantage of other companies usually have a reputation for doing so. Use your network of associates or other companies to see how they treat other companies. If you feel you have to deal with a company with a sinister past, go armed and forewarned.

- The vast majority of larger companies are not interested in stealing your property. The potential liabilities for doing so far outweigh any gain they could have in almost every case. Be aware that they do see a lot of opportunities, though, and will not always be responsive to your effort to protect your property. Getting to know the company and the people who work there will help you decide how to proceed when they ask to see proprietary property.

- One of the best ways for you to deal with a large company is to understand the company from their own perspective. Usually breakdowns in negotiations have more to do with a lack of understanding by one or the other party than they do with the substance of the deal. You can avoid many problems by doing your homework and knowing who you are dealing with.

- Keep an open mind. Just because one company does something one way doesn't mean that is the only way to do it. Creativity and flexibility are often provide the ideal solution to problems.

- Always keep the end goal in sight. Before any negotiation, remind yourself why you are there and what your primary objective is. Don't get so caught up in the details that you miss the opportunity to make things work.

Protecting yourself and your company is important. If you understand how to effectively protect your company and its property, you will feel much more comfortable talking to larger companies and any other potential partner as well. There will always be hard choices, but demonstrating that you understand things like patents, trademarks, copyrights, trade secrets, and contracts will generate respect and help to put the other party on notice that you are aware of the issues and they had better be, too.

Chapter 4

Understanding How Large Companies Think and Operate

Why should I work to understand my large business counterpart? Isn't the language of business universal, regardless of size? Don't we all speak the same language and have the same basic objectives? Are small businesses and large businesses really all that different in the way they think and the way they operate from day to day?

Before we answer these questions, let's change the scenario a bit. What if we were not trying to partner with a large company, but instead we were simply trying to take our products into a new marketplace in a foreign country. What if we ask the same basic questions and receive the following answers?

Question 1: Why should I work to understand my foreign business counterpart? Is it really going to make a difference?

Answer: I don't think we need to spend a lot of effort to get to know our customer or the foreign marketplace. At the end of the day it's all about product, price, and service. If we have the best product at the best price and the best service, we will get the deal regardless of how well we understand each other.

Question 2: Isn't the language of business universal, regardless of location? Don't we all speak the same language and have the same basic objectives?

Answer: They speak English and we speak English, seems good enough for me.

Question 3: Are businesses in [our Country] and businesses in [Foreign Country] really all that different in the way they think and the way they operate from day to day?

Answer: Forget culture. Business is business regardless of the culture. I can't imagine how we could really be that different anyway. We need to move forward. Forget the touchy feely stuff. I'm sure they [the customer] feel the same way.

If you were the CEO of a company and this was the response you got from your senior salesperson, what would you do? Would you agree? Would you start looking for another salesperson?

Most of us would start looking for another salesperson because we know very well the importance of understanding our customer and we clearly understand that cultural misunderstandings have ruined many a deal, regardless of price, quality, and/or service. Further, even if we both speak English, we know how important it is that we take the time to really understand each other before we come to a binding agreement.

These principles of understanding are fundamental common sense and basic business practice when dealing with international customers. And yet, we often see small businesses make these basic mistakes. Too often, small businesses jump to the conclusion that just because both parties are in the same business, they fully understand each other. And just because they have good prices, quality, and service, they will automatically seal the deal. Consequently, many small businesses are very surprised when they think they did everything right but everything ends so wrong.

Do small businesses really operate that differently from large businesses? Yes and no. Do American businesses really operate that differently from Japanese businesses? The answer is the same, yes and no. In both cases, each business fundamentally runs the same way. Yet in very specific ways each runs quite differently. Like cultural differences, the answer is always in the details. All humans eat and sleep, and yet many wars have been fought because of basic misunderstandings of much less important matters. Similarly, although all businesses operate fundamentally the same way at the macro level, they operate much differently at the more detailed level. Consequently, the more we work to understand each other, the better the chance that we will avert problems later on. With this in mind, let's consider some typical areas of concern.

Three Basic Frustrations of Partnering with Large Companies

My first job out of college was as a mid-level manager for a company with sales of approximately $50 million per year. Although the company was publicly held, family members held more than 50 percent of the stock and filled almost all of the senior management positions. At first I reported to a non-family member. However within a few years, I was fortunate enough to report directly to one of the largest shareholders and the most influential member of the senior management team.

I truly enjoyed working for this man. He had incredibly good business judgment and tremendous communication skills. He was a man of integrity. He taught me a lot about working with people and how to cut through red tape to get things done. He took me under his wing and taught me how to run a business. It was a great education for a young manager.

While this reporting relationship enabled me to get an early introduction to the thought processes of senior management and the intricacies of managing people, it completely distorted my view of the way many large companies operate. As a middle manager reporting directly to one of the most influential shareholders, I had no worries about the way other departments would be affected, no worries about shareholder backlash, and no worries about other senior management opinions. Decisions were made very quickly and even budgets were somewhat flexible if we determined that circumstances merited a change in direction. We could even take some risks with customer opinion if we believed we were doing the right thing in the end.

With that background, you can imagine my surprise and frustration when I went to work for large corporations. I was used to making quick decisions without a lot of input from others and I had grown accustomed to making "right" decisions regardless of conflicting policies or rules. Don't get me wrong—I didn't see myself as a cowboy. My mentor had taught me the importance of following reporting lines and of honoring corporate policies and budgets. However, in a much smaller business, my reporting line was one level deep, which meant we could always move very quickly when we saw a good opportunity.

I soon became frustrated with the pace and rigidity of large corporations. I saw them as ineffective and inefficient. In my mind, it was a failure on the part of corporate leadership. For a time, I considered staying completely away from the corporate world. The thing that kept me involved was my curiosity as to how they could be so inefficient and still grow so large and be so profitable. Now, 20 years later, I see many small business owners following the same learning curve. They become frustrated and impatient with the way large companies work, which leads to actions and decisions that ultimately kill the partnership. Let's consider three primary misunderstandings that have stopped many a deal from occurring.

Slow Decision Making

I think one of the hardest things to get used to when working with a large corporation is the amount of time it seems to take to make decisions. Small businesses can make relatively major decisions in days or weeks, while large corporations will often take months and can even take years to make some major decisions. This seemingly slow process can be exasperating to the small business manager who is used to making decisions much more quickly, and who is often very anxious to move forward with the deal. Occasionally, smaller business managers interpret slow decision making as a lack of interest. This often leads them to either over-sell or under-price the deal in an attempt to speed things along. They may even walk away from a good deal based on this erroneous understanding.

If the large organization is a company, bureaucracy (government), university, or any other large entity with a hierarchal form of management, then you will likely see a lot of effort trying to convince other members of the organization that partnering with your company is a good idea. Usually large organizations have systems for getting approval of new projects. These systems will likely involve multiple layers of management and may span several departments. Getting approval takes time and patience.

So Many Decision Makers

You're not going to change the fact that there are many decision makers in a large company. Rather than getting frustrated, accept the fact that many people will review your project, and take the time to get to know as many of these people as you can. They are likely people you may be working with in the future in some capacity or other, and taking time during the decision making process to get to know them will payoff later when you are working together.

It takes a lot longer to get to know a large company than it does a small company. One advantage of longer lead times on decisions is that it gives you time to learn about your potential partner before you make the deal with them. You can spend time getting to know who all the managers are and how things work within the company. Taking time to learn about your potential partner will give you a better understanding of how to work with them after the deal is made. There is a great likelihood that the same process that controls whether a partnership deal is done or not is similar to how all project modifications or approvals are done.

Overemphasis on the Budget

Large organizations can seemingly focus too much on staying within the budget. They have been known to walk away from or delay "really good deals" based on budget concerns. And heaven forbid any attempt to modify a budget in the middle of the fiscal year, regardless of the reason. Depending on the level of the person involved, they may even be stuck on meeting a single line item on the budget, even though the partnership would improve the overall budget performance. This apparent rigid adherence to the budget can be very frustrating to the small business manager who has grown his/her business by being flexible and aggressive. They see this lack of flexibility as bureaucratic and perhaps even downright foolish while the large company sees it as an inviolate part of running the business.

From the Larger Business Perspective

Certainly, each of these issues can be a frustration to the small business manager as they develop a relationship with a potential partner. Sometimes, they become such a frustration that the small business manager simply walks away from the deal. As mentioned earlier, it is easy to misinterpret these characteristics as a lack of interest or desire on the part of the large company management team, which can lead small business managers to wrong conclusions.

What we don't know is that, on any given day, each of these issues is also a frustration to the people who work in these large organizations. Sometimes they are even more frustrated than their counterpart in the small business. No one likes slow decision making, too many decision makers, and overemphasis on budgets. Many books have been written about how to correct or eliminate each of these problems. Most major corporations expend significant efforts to develop processes to speed decision making, streamline lines of authority, and ensure that long term strengths are not sacrificed for short term budget considerations. Yet, despite all of that effort, even the best large organizations are lumbering giants compared to their more nimble small business counterparts.

So what should the small business manager do? Should they stop pushing and simply sit back and wait? Of course not! You don't grow from small to large by sitting back and waiting. You need to keep moving forward, but you need to move forward in a smart and professional way. So how do we keep things moving while keeping our cool? What is it about our large business counterpart we need to understand?

First, one needs to recognize that a certain amount of bureaucracy is necessary to protect the interests of both parties. For example, consider what would happen if the small company delivers a poor quality product that results in significant negative publicity and customer lawsuits? The results could be disastrous for both parties. The small company could be sued and perhaps even go out of business, while the larger company could lose brand loyalty they have worked a generation to create. They could be faced with litigation expenses for years to come, not to mention the lost market share, revenues, and profits that will certainly result.

Bureaucracy seems to follow any large organization. The reason is quite simple. It takes a lot of work to keep a large organization running effectively. It isn't just that a lot of people need to be on the same page with company objectives; entire divisions or subsidiaries have to be kept on the same page. Large companies employ thousands of people. To keep that many people organized there has to be a power structure and a communication system. The larger the company, the more functional groups the company is likely to have. All these have to communicate with each other and work with each other. To do this there also has to be paper trails to keep track of intercompany interaction. If one division needs supplies from another division, the movement of those supplies must be recorded. These systems will likely use things like purchase orders and invoices with specific approval processes. While it might seem like a lot of red tape to the small business owner, it is a very necessary part of running a large business.

Large businesses also have to contend with a number of human resource issues that smaller businesses don't, such as affirmative action, minority business ownership, insurance, and government-mandated employee benefits. Depending on the type of partnership you establish, some of these issues may carry over to their obligations and they will likely ask a number of questions about your company because of it.

To a lesser extent the same scenario could be played out when a smaller partner cannot handle the increased volume, did not adequately protect patents, trademarks, or copyrights, participated in illegal hiring practices, operated in an unsafe manner, and so on. In each case, the penalty can be significant. Yet, in most cases, the smaller company will want to move forward. To them, the rewards far outweigh the risks. However, what about the large company? They already have name recognition, brand loyalty, and a solid customer base. How do they perceive the risk/reward equation? If they do not do an adequate job of due diligence, they could be risking hundreds of millions of dollars and thousands of jobs, not to mention the goodwill they have created over decades. Unless the deal is completely safe and a no-brainer, they have a clear responsibility to their shareholders, customers, and employees to slow down and make sure things are done right.

Second, while multiple decision makers can be a hindrance to speed, they can also be an aid to quality and ultimate success. Some of the most successful organizations are notoriously slow when it comes to making critical decisions. They seek many opinions from many different business units and departments to fully vet the consequences and benefits of any potential business transaction. Yes, it can be exasperating sometimes. And yet, these companies seldom make a big mistake. When they go to market with a new idea, it almost always works because the entire organization is behind it. When they select a partner in this manner, the partnership almost always works and often lasts for decades. In the end, most small companies would rather have a lasting relationship that works for both parties than a quick deal that soon fizzles with unforeseen problems and lack of internal support.

Third, goal setting and budgets are an integral part of maintaining control of the company. Large corporations have literally tens of thousands of employees, divisions all over the world, hundreds if not thousands of products, and contracts with thousands of suppliers and/or partners. Can you imagine the result if budgets were just guidelines and not rules? Consider what would happen if half of the managers decided, on their own, to overspend their budget by just 20 percent under the guise that they were simply doing the "right" thing for the long term. Obviously, the result could be disastrous. Profits would be seriously reduced. Shareholders would lose confidence in the company. Capital sources would begin to dry up and costs would rise. Managers would be unclear about expectations. Suppliers and partners could go unpaid and employees could be let go. The result would be chaos. Even if all of the ideas were ultimately proven to be good ideas, it is doubtful that the organization could survive the lack of control.

With that as a backdrop, it is important for a smaller company to see that strict budget controls are their friend, not their enemy. Companies with strict budget guidelines typically pay their bills, honor their commitments, and are still around for the long haul. Companies that play fast and loose are just that—fast and loose. They run out of cash fast and they consider your contract very loose. You will likely find that the slower companies tend to plan better and have a greater consistency when it comes to paying their bills on time. I would much rather have a company that pays in 60 days rather than one that says they pay right away but then doesn't because they have cash problems.

Recently I heard about a company in my industry that got this large contract from a new company. The new company seemed to have everything going for it. They were paying big money to get good partners so they could quickly rise to the top. After they started the project, the company had to hire many extra workers. They put all these people on their payroll and then the new company lost its investors as the project was nearing completion. It was a disaster. The new company folded and pulled the other company down with it.

Trust between partners is important. Just remember that the time it takes to get budgets approved is time well spent, if it means a greater likelihood that the money for the partnership will be there when it is needed.

Hopefully each of these examples provides some insight into the way large companies think and operate, and particularly in how they think differently from a small organization. Why is it important to understand how they think? What difference does it make? Really, it makes all the difference. Put yourself in the shoes of the large organization. Would you want to do business with a small company that does not appreciate the importance of due diligence in determining the viability of their partners, that does not appreciate the value of getting multiple opinions before proceeding with a major decision, or that feels that budgets are simply guidelines that can be broken whenever necessary? Of course you wouldn't! And yet, many small businesses portray just that attitude. They almost see it as a badge of honor to be a rough rider among a group of farmers. They forget that rough riders come in fast and go away just as quickly, while the farmer continues to prosper from year to year.

The key word when it comes to working with a large company is patience. Large companies run on a different clock than small companies. Everything will likely take longer. Don't lose heart. Just be patient and try to learn the process. If you take the time to learn how things work in the large business, you will be able to monitor the process. It is like trying to rush through a traffic jam. If you push too hard, you will likely crash. If you are patient and let the cars clear out, you will likely get to your destination.

What Large Companies Fear the Most

Sometimes we think of large companies as being powerful and absolutely fearless. With hundreds of millions of dollars and thousands of employees, what could they possibly fear? And yet every large corporation has three common fears. The better we understand these fears, the better we can proactively address them in our negotiations and show the large company that we share their fears as well. The truth is that fear drives many decisions in business regardless of the size of that business. Anyone who has experience working in a large company will tell you that fear drives many decisions. The larger the company, the more that company has to lose. If a big company fails, it means thousands of jobs lost instead of a couple dozen. Most large companies take very seriously the fact that their success is critical to the well-being of the thousands of people they employ.

The Fear of Negative Publicity

Most large corporations will do almost anything to avoid negative publicity. They will spend millions of dollars, and they will even walk away from seemingly good deals if there is any possibility of negative publicity. Negative publicity can come in many ways:

- A corporate spokesperson commits an offensive or illegal act.
- The corporation is accused of participating in predatory or unfair business practices.
- Product quality is shown to be problematic, or worse, criminally negligent.
- The company is accused of illegal and/or discriminatory hiring practices.
- The company is accused of sexual harassment.
- The company is accused of evading taxes.
- The company is accused of illegal environmental practices.
- The company is accused of improper relations with public officials.

Why is negative publicity such a problem? When a company has serious problems with negative publicity, five things occur. Let's look at each one:

Customer Loyalty Decreases: When a company receives negative publicity, the company will quickly notice a serious drop in customer loyalty. After all, who wants to be associated with a pariah? When this happens, three things occur: 1) Customers are less willing to stock the product; 2) Consumer confidence wanes; 3) Brand equity is damaged.

Stock Prices Drop: The stock market almost always reacts very quickly. Consequently, three things happen as a result: 1) Shareholders become dissatisfied; 2) Leadership feel less than secure; 3) Capital becomes harder to raise.

Costs Increase: In order to maintain market share and regain credibility, the company is then 1) Forced to spend more on advertising; 2) Expend more for sales team effort; 3) Spend more for public relations repairs.

Loss of Morale: As profits dry up, so do bonuses, etc. Consequently, 1) Key employees depart; 2) It becomes more difficult to attract talented employees; 3) Those who remain are less motivated.

Competitors Are Emboldened: When competitors see weakness, they then begin working to 1) Grab your market share; 2) Advertise directly against you; 3) Try to hire your key employees.

This downward spiral continues until the leadership team can turn things around. Sometimes this takes months, years, even decades. The diagram in Figure 4.1 depicts this downward cycle.

A company that I was working with had a problem with negative publicity. Word got out that the company was having financial problems because a disgruntled vendor didn't get paid. Even though the company settled things with the vendor, the damage was already done. The news caused many of the company vendors to start to question the company. Some of them asked for new terms for their deals with the company. Other partners of the company were more reluctant to do business with the company. It took a long time to clean up the damage.

Larger companies may want to see your own efforts to avoid negative publicity. They may also want to see how you might have handled it in the past. If a small company seems to have a devil-may-care attitude toward bad publicity, it will cause many larger companies to pause. While the company may be an excellent partner, the larger company will not be willing to take on the additional liability.

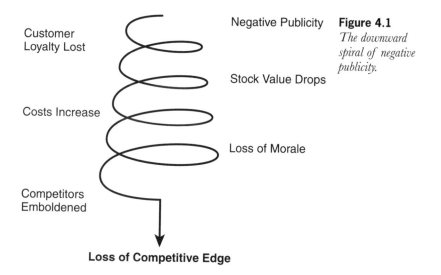

Figure 4.1
The downward spiral of negative publicity.

The Fear of Lost Market Share (or Competitive Edge)

Market share is a measure of relative performance against your competitors. It measures what percentage of the market your company currently enjoys. For example, Delta Airlines has a larger market share than Jet Blue because more passengers fly with Delta than with Jet Blue. Procter and Gamble has a larger market share of laundry detergents (Tide, Cheer, Gain, Era, etc.) than Henkel (Purex) because more people buy Procter and Gamble detergents than Henkel detergents. A company can be seen in a positive light and yet still be losing market share, though, so why is this measure so important to corporate America?

1. Market share is a good measure of performance against competitors. If market share is being lost, then the public prefers the competitive product to your product for some reason. Your competitors are doing something right, and you are doing something wrong.

2. Ongoing and systemic loss of market share is typically a sign that prices are too high, quality is inferior, advertising is inadequate, and so on. If something is not done about it, the company risks becoming inconsequential in the marketplace.

3. Consumer goods retailers will reduce shelf space for the lower share products, which leads to ongoing loss of volume, revenue, and profits.

4. Ongoing and systemic loss of market share indicates a company in decline, which leads to reduced stock prices, changes in management, and so on.

Recognize that market share is typically measured by brand as well as in total (as suggested in the detergent example). A single company may have several brands that compete against each other for individual market share while at the same time contributing to the company's total market share. A brand manager may be assigned to a specific brand and would therefore have all of the same concerns at the brand level that a marketing vice president would have for the entire corporation. Why is this important to know? Because even though your partnership may boost total company market share, it may cannibalize specific brands' market share. Therefore, you may have a friend at the corporate level and an "enemy" at the brand level. Understanding how your product or service affects market share will help you determine where and how to sell your partnership within the corporation.

The Fear of Civil Litigation or Criminal Prosecution

This fear is more than fear of negative publicity. This fear is one of jail time, public humiliation, and/or significant catastrophic losses to the business due to civil penalties. Why should large companies worry about these items? Because they are real; we hear about it nearly every day in the news somewhere. Certainly, many of the offenders are truly guilty and deserve the penalties they receive. However, it should also be noted that attorney generals seldom get a lot of public praise for prosecuting the little guy, and newspapers seldom sell a lot of papers by putting a sole proprietor on the front page of their paper. However, just the opposite is true with a large company CEO. With this in mind, large organizations expend literally millions of dollars each year to settle or avoid lawsuits. To them, it is simply a cost of doing business.

Large companies that mass-market their products to consumers can have huge liabilities if one of their products is proven to be defective or harmful. In the mid-1990s, Wyeth was marketing a diet aid called Fen-Phen, (fenfluramine and phentermine). The two drugs were effective at weight reduction, but one of the drugs—fenfluramine—was found to cause heart valve problems and pulmonary hypertension, both of which can be fatal. Even though the products were pulled from the shelves, Wyeth was left with a disaster. Not only was there severe damage to the company's reputation, but there was evidence of people dying from the drug. Lawsuits were inevitable, and they came in droves totaling more than 50,000 product liability lawsuits. While some of the cases are still being sorted out, it is estimated that the total product liability is more than $14 billion. Wyeth announced that it set aside $21.1 billion to cover the costs of the lawsuits.

While your company and your potential partner may not have to deal with a product liability case of the magnitude that Wyeth had to deal with, the Wyeth story is chilling. I am not saying that the lawsuits were not justified. The drugs were dangerous, and they did harm a lot of people. However, there is plenty of evidence that once the floodgates were open, there was also a significant amount of fraud in some of the alleged cases. The settlements were only part of the money the company had to spend. There were also significant attorney fees and a substantial amount of time spent dealing with all of the cases.

The mere mention of a class action tort like the one Wyeth came up against can cause fear in any company that sells its products to a large audience. The bigger the company and the larger the market, the more exposure there is to these types of lawsuits. Companies can't afford that type of exposure, so they go to great lengths to avoid anything that even remotely resembles a product liability situation. For this reason, a large company will be interested in your company's product testing procedures and practices. If they see that you are as careful as they are about your products, you can win friends. If they feel your approach to product testing is insufficient, they may have problems with a partnership.

So why should the small business manager care about these fears? Don't we all have them, in one way or another? Of course we do. To a large organization, though, these fears are much greater than to a small organization because there is so much more to lose. Failure on the part of the small business owner to address these fears will be a deal breaker almost all of the time. If a senior executive of a large corporation has the slightest concern that negative publicity could even possibly occur as a result of your partnership, they will almost always shy away from the deal. The same will be true of any possibility of lost market share, civil litigation, and criminal prosecution. The small business person may feel that the probability of any of these is minimal and hence worth the risk. They may feel that the large business manager is being ridiculously cautious and overly risk adverse. However, they will seldom win this argument. And they may even lose the deal by marginalizing these concerns (particularly with senior management). The better approach is to do whatever you have to do to ensure that the partnership has near zero probability that any of these concerns could actually come to pass. On the other hand, if you can show that the partnership has a high likelihood of generating positive publicity or of increasing market share, you will certainly increase your odds of success.

Little Fiefdoms

Another big difference between small businesses and large businesses is the existence of various departments within the company. Depending on the size and complexity of the business, these departments may be almost completely autonomous from each other. In fact, in many cases, they even appear to be very competitive.

Some companies encourage competition between departments as a way to incentivize them to higher performance. Some companies, while they may not encourage internal competition, still have systems where groups within the organization have to compete for resources or funding. Even if it isn't formal competition, there can still be an undercurrent of competition because everyone knows that money is tight or limited.

With any organized power structure, there will be people who have responsibility over parts of the organization. Even though the company may preach teamwork and sharing, there will likely still be a sense of ownership and territorialism. This isn't always bad, but it can cause an "us versus them" attitude to develop within the company between functioning groups or divisions.

Consider this example from one of our clients:

- The company had more than 100,000 employees and more than $40 billion in annual sales.

- The business was broken into four geographical regions (North America, Latin America, Europe, and Asia). Each region was led by an Executive Vice President responsible for profit and loss.

- The North American region was broken into five divisions based on the product line. Each of these was led by a Senior Vice President responsible for profit and loss of that division.

- Each division had several business units (18 in total), and each business unit was led by a Vice President/General Manager responsible for profit and loss.

- The business units in North America were supported by more than 50 manufacturing facilities who reported to Plant Managers, Directors, Vice Presidents, and an Executive Vice President equal in authority to the Regional Vice Presidents.

- In addition to these executives, the company had more than 50 other Vice Presidents, Senior Vice Presidents, and Executive Vice Presidents responsible for various support functions and the like.

- In total there were well over 300 people who had the title of Director or Vice President.

Now picture trying to sell a global engagement to this group. Each Vice President has profit and loss responsibility and each has differing priorities and needs. In many cases, they have conflicting objectives that must be addressed. Although they are part of one large company, inside the business they can appear to be much more like little fiefdoms, each vying for resources, recognition, power, and control.

Small companies often underestimate the complexity of dealing with a large organization, and they very typically fail to recognize the intense competition between senior managers who are vying for corporate resources and corporate recognition. One minute they think they are sailing along nicely, and the next minute they are on a sinking ship. They did not even see the torpedo in the water. Often, they do not even understand the reporting relationship from one manager to another. Consequently, they fail to recognize those people who can make or break the deal.

With this in mind, it is highly recommended that the small business take time to fully understand the organizational design of the large business and to obtain as much information as possible about the reporting relationship of each senior manager, particularly which level typically makes the final decision. Here are a few things to consider:

- There is almost always competition between business unit leaders, if not for resources, then at least for recognition. While the managers may be friendly and positive toward each other, the small business should never get caught giving one more consideration or attention than another.

- Recognize the difference between a business unit leader and a functional leader. Typically, the business unit leader will have more power than the functional leader in that the business unit leader has profit/loss responsibility, while the other may simply be considered a "cost" center.

- Business unit leaders will be more prone to bend budget rules because they are more accountable for bottom line performance than for line item budget items. Therefore, if you are proposing a solution that clearly affects the bottom line but negatively affects a portion of the budget, you may want to involve the business unit leader.

- Avoid getting in the crossfire between sales, marketing, and operations. There is often friction between these groups. If you have to take sides, be prepared for the torpedo. It will be coming. Work to address both sides' concerns before pitching the solution.

Big Dog–Little Dog

My daughter has a wonderful dog named Bella. Bella has a ton of energy and she commands attention wherever she goes. She loves people and people love her. We throw a football or a Frisbee to her and she brings it back. She rides a surfboard in the pool and she chases the deer in our back yard. She goes running with my son-in-law and she strikes fear in the heart of the local cats.

Now guess what kind of dog she is: an Australian Shepherd, a Golden Retriever, a Doberman? No! Bella is a Malti-poo. Sopping wet, I think she may weigh six or seven pounds. Yet, in her mind, she is as big as any big dog. She even barks like a big dog when someone comes to the door. Occasionally, she even tries to mix it up with the big dogs. While we may treat her like a big dog and sometimes we even think of her like a big dog, in the end, she is a little dog.

Some corporate managers can be a bit like Bella. They want you to believe they are the big dog. They bark like a big dog and act like a big dog, and if you didn't know better, you would think they are the big dog, but really they are just a little dog. Therefore, as you work to develop a partnership, it is important to know exactly who you are dealing with. How much authority do they have? How much respect in the organization do they have? How well connected are they to the decision maker? Do they have influence in the decision making process? Finding answers to these questions can be the difference between making the deal and losing the deal and between wasting time and money or investing time and money wisely.

So how do you know whether you are working with a big dog or a little dog, and what should you do about it? Should you always try to work with senior management? How do you move up the corporate ladder while maintaining positive relationships with the middle manager? Obviously, the answer depends on a number of factors. In Chapters 5 and 6 we discuss ways to reach the decision maker and ways to maintain good relationships with each of the people you meet along the way. For now, let's discuss how to determine the decision making ability of the person you are working with along with the typical characteristics of middle and senior level managers.

You can save yourself a lot of frustration and potential embarrassment by simply doing your homework before you ever meet your contact. Here are some ideas to help you determine your contact's influence before you even make the first visit:

- If the company is publicly held, find their annual report and get the names and titles of their corporate officers. It is not uncommon for an annual report to list senior management two to three levels below the CEO. Is your contact on this list? What is his/her title?

- You can Google the person's name. Most senior level managers will show up somewhere. Perhaps they have given a speech somewhere? Perhaps they are on another corporation's Board of Directors. You would be surprised what you can find by simply doing an internet search. You will likely find something if the person has very much influence in the business.

- If you have other contacts in the business, call them. Depending on your relationship with them, they may be able to tell you a lot about the group or individual you will be visiting.

- Do you have other friends or contacts that have done business with this corporation? What can they tell you?

Here are some ways to determine the decision making authority of the person you will be working with during your first contact/visit:

- Ask for a business card and pay particular attention to the job title. In most large corporations, titles such as Director, Senior Director, Vice President, General Manager, Chief Operating Officer, Chief Financial Officer, and Chief Executive Officer are decision makers or potential decision makers. Titles such as Manager, Foreman, Analyst, and the like may have influence, but they are probably not the final decision maker. Here are some thoughts on a few of the various titles you might see in an organization:

  - Manager of Systems Administration—Probably not a decision maker; appears to be an administrative function.

  - Director of Sales or Operations—Clearly has line authority; depending on the amount of money involved he/she may be the decision maker. This person will at least heavily influence the decision.

  - Vice President–Procurement—Are you selling something procurement will directly use? If not, this person is a gatekeeper. He/she may have influence and may ultimately do the negotiation, but is not the decision maker.

  - Executive Assistant to the President—Be careful. This person may be a gatekeeper, but will likely have a lot more power than you might expect. If they like you, they can arrange meetings with the right people. If they don't, you're in trouble.

- Vice President/General Manager—Decision maker or strong influence on the decision.

- Manager of Corporate Strategy—Hard to tell strength in the organization. Probably not a decision maker, but he/she may have strong influence.

- Manager of Corporate Brands—Probably not a decision maker, but may have some influence.

- Director of Corporate Brands—Likely a decision maker or at least will contribute to the decision.

- Set the stage that you would like to get to know the company better before making a formal presentation, and create a written agenda for your questions. Ask about product lines, distribution channels, and so on. Include a question about organizational structure. Sometimes they will just give you the organizational chart.

- If you suspect the contact to be middle management or below, ask the contact to go to lunch or dinner with you before the initial visit as an informal way to get to know them and the company better. During lunch you can ask questions about how the company works, pitfalls to watch out for, and so on. If appropriate, ask how decisions are typically made and for suggestions of dos and don'ts during the formal visit. Most middle managers will be flattered that you respect their opinion in this way and will be happy to give you helpful pointers. This will help them save face when they ultimately inform you that they are not the decision maker. Never ask the person directly if they have the authority to make the decision; try to ascertain that information while maintaining a good relationship with that person.

- In group session or in private, at some point simply ask your contact for advice on how best to move the process along. Let them know that you don't want to offend anyone or waste anyone's time unnecessarily, you simply want to meet their expectations. Do the decision makers like Power Point presentations? Do they simply like to ask questions? Would they like to visit your facility? What is the style of the decision maker? Very formal, less formal, very time conscious, suggested dress code, and so on. Most people will appreciate the fact that you can tailor your presentation to the needs of the audience and they like the fact that you are involving them in the method of presentation. If possible, work to involve the initial contact in the presentation, even if it is to simply acknowledge their help and assistance in bringing this opportunity to the company's attention.

Understanding Middle Managers versus Senior Managers

In order to move things to a positive conclusion, it is important to understand the difference between the way middle managers think and operate versus the way senior management think and operate. Recognize that you will likely need to interact on a regular basis with both levels of management. How you interact with them will make a very large impact on the ultimate success or failure of the partnership. Here are some ideas in regard to each level of management.

Middle managers:

- Generally are still trying to move up the ladder and are very career conscious. They will often think first about the way this will affect their career and second about the way this will affect the bottom line of the company. Therefore, be very sensitive to ensure that your contact sees this as helpful to his/her career aspirations.

- Generally see adherence to company policies as inviolate rules. They will be reluctant to support anything that is in conflict with current corporate policies or procedures.

- Similarly see adherence to budget as not optional. They will be reluctant to support anything that leads to overspending of the current budget.

- As mentioned earlier, they will want to know how this will be presented and whether this will likely make them look good or bad. Work to involve them in the presentation wherever possible. Particularly ensure that they do not feel you are using them to get to senior management and will then toss them aside. Make sure they know that you will treat them with the same respect after the partnership as before the partnership.

- Generally are focused more on the short term than senior management is. However, they do see the big picture and do want to do the right thing for the long term. Sometimes they do not articulate this as well.

- Usually have more time to work with you than senior management will have. Use this time to develop a relationship, practice presentations, seek advice, enlist their help and suggestions, and so on.

Senior management:

- Typically see the bigger picture and are more willing to take risks.

- Will bend the rules if they feel there is significant upside potential.

- Have a larger budget to work with and more budget freedom.

- May be willing to invest for the long term if they are on track for current quarterly and yearly performance targets.

- Will not invest for the long term if they are under significant pressure to deliver quarterly and yearly performance targets.

- Have a lot of things pitched at them. They typically ask a lot of tough questions and are skeptical. Be very well prepared and be flexible in your presentation approach.

- Have bigger egos and are more conscious of their time. They will generally act busy, even if they are not that busy. Clearly ask how much time you have to work with and then make sure to stay within that time limit. If the meeting starts late, still work to end on time.

- Like to ask questions and talk. Don't overload your presentation. Allow for and encourage participation and questions throughout the presentation. They don't like to listen to another pitch, they want you to listen to them and show them how you understand their needs and how you can meet their needs.

- Trust some middle managers more than others. Do your homework here and make sure you know the decision makers and the strong influencers.

- Generally understand the importance of integrity. They like to work with people they can trust.

- Will strongly avoid negative publicity or litigation. Make it clear that this will not occur.

- Make judgments quickly. It is very difficult to get a second chance if you fail the first one.

- Will walk away from good deals if negotiations get overly bitter, trust is lost, or numbers and terms start to change after a verbal agreement is made. Be very careful what you say or promise. Most senior managers are very smart and have very good memories.

- Typically see opportunities in the millions and tens of millions of dollar ranges, so they will not listen to or get excited about "small" deals. Therefore, it is important to match the size of the deal to the decision making authority of the person making the deal. If your deal is worth about one million per year and a Director can sign that agreement, then don't take it to the Vice President.

- Will not typically let your attorney create the legal documents. They will work to ensure the documents are fairly written, but they will not risk litigation because of poorly written agreements by your attorney.

- Generally desire win/win arrangements. They do not want to go through this again with another partner next year. Therefore, they will sometimes leave money on the table in order to work with someone they trust and have confidence in. Always ensure that the senior manager's trust is honored and respected. If you lose their confidence or trust, no amount of price negotiation will keep you in the deal.

Speaking the Language

A few years ago a large multinational client asked me to visit a couple of business units they had in France. It should have been no big deal. I had already visited business units in Singapore, Brussels, and Frankfurt with no problems. And yet I really did not want to go on this trip. I knew that I would pretty well be on my own and I didn't speak a word of French. I had heard horror stories about how the French people viewed Americans. Frankly, I had visions of getting lost in the country and having absolutely no help whatsoever.

One day a few weeks before the trip, I mentioned these fears to a friend of mine. He laughed and made a suggestion. "Spend a little time learning some basic French phrases, and everything will go wonderfully." I thought he must be joking, but he seemed dead serious. So I thought, why not? It can't possibly hurt. I practiced my few phrases over the next few weeks. Then at the appointed time, I got on the airplane and flew into Lyon. My first encounter was at the car rental counter. I simply greeted the person in French, apologized for my poor French ability, and then spoke English for the rest of the conversation. Imagine my surprise when the person went out of her way to help me. She couldn't have been more helpful. Later at the hotel, I did the same thing, with the same result. I did the same at dinner and so on throughout the three day visit. I met at least 50 perfect strangers and every one of them was as kind and gracious as I have ever experienced. Even those who spoke little English went out of their way to help me.

So what made the difference? Did I completely misjudge the people and culture of an entire country? Yes, I think I did misjudge the French people, and I also learned a very important lesson. When I at least tried to acknowledge their native language and culture and apologized for not knowing it better, people went out of their way to help me. I don't know if they liked Americans or disliked Americans, but I do know that when I showed respect for their language and culture they responded in like kind.

In a similar way, small business managers need to at least make an attempt to understand the language of large businesses. They don't have to be fluent, but they do need to be able to carry a conversation.

So what is the language of large business? The language of business is really pretty basic. It revolves around 10 key measures. If you understand these measures and why they are important, you will be able to at least communicate with each other.

Return on Invested Capital (ROIC) and/or Return on Investment (ROI)

ROIC measures the company's ability to generate positive returns on the capital under its control. The formula for this is generally

$$ROIC = \frac{Net\ Income - Dividends}{Total\ Capital}$$

If we break this into more detail, the formula would look like the following:

$$ROIC = \frac{Revenue - Cost\ of\ Goods\ Sold - Overhead - Dividends}{Fixed\ Assets + Working\ Capital}$$

This measure basically tells shareholders and other potential investors what kind of return the company is getting on its capital investments, and it is a good indicator of the financial health of the company. The higher the return, the more people will want to invest. The lower the return, the less people will want to invest.

Similarly, *ROI* measures the company's expected return on a single investment. The formula for this measure is

$$ROI = \frac{(Gain\ from\ Investment - Cost\ of\ Investment)}{Cost\ of\ Investment}$$

So why does this matter to the small business manager who wants to partner with the large company? The answer is simple: Almost every large company measures investments against this formula or a formula like it. They will be comparing the potential return on investment for your deal with the return on investment of other deals. If your opportunity provides a higher return on capital investment, then it will likely get more consideration. If it does not provide a strong return, then it will typically not see the light of day.

Revenue and Volume Growth

This measure simply monitors sales growth from month to month and from year to year. Sales growth is another good indicator of the health of the organization. In many large organizations, revenue and volume growth are watched very closely. And senior management spend significant portions of their time in efforts to boost revenue growth from quarter to quarter. Why does this matter to the small business partner? If your idea or proposal can be shown to have a high probability of generating more revenue, it will get immediate attention from the key decision makers of the business.

Profit Growth

Similar to revenue and volume, *profit growth* is closely monitored from month to month, quarter to quarter, and year to year. Therefore, any idea or proposal that significantly improves profits will also command a lot of attention. The proposal may reduce costs and hence improve profits, or it may boost sales and therefore profits. Regardless of the approach, the small business person would be wise to analyze the proposal against its effect on bottom line profits.

Market Share

Market share is another indicator of a company's competitiveness and overall health. Therefore, it is watched very carefully by most members of senior management. Small business managers need to be certain that their product or service will not harm overall market share. Additionally, as mentioned, small business managers need to be on the look-out for specific brand managers with specific market share objectives. You will find an ally in any brand manager who is helped by your product or service. And you will find just the opposite in any brand manager who is adversely affected by your product or service.

Customer Service

Large corporations have many ways of measuring customer service, including line item fill rate, order fill rate, order shipped complete, perfect order, and many other derivations. This measure is typically watched very closely because it is a major indicator of how well the operations side of the business is meeting customer orders. Salespeople dislike having to call customers who are complaining of delivery issues. It takes time, it is a negative experience, and it detracts from their ability to sell other products or promotions. Operations dislike having to deal with sales complaints and the increased costs associated with correcting problems. Customer service measures are almost always a bone of contention between sales and operations, with each pointing the finger at the other for the root cause. With this in mind, the small business person will need to make certain that their proposal does not adversely affect customer service. If the proposal is designed to boost sales volume, make sure that operational concerns are addressed. As mentioned earlier, this is an area where the torpedo is typically already in the water. Sales may love the idea, while operations sends in the torpedo because of fears relative to customer service. The opposite can occur with a proposal that aids operations in the reduction of costs but adds complexity for the customer or even detracts from overall delivery performance.

Working Capital

Working capital consists of current assets (cash, current accounts receivable, turning inventory) minus current accounts payable. Sometimes the measure is referred to as *operating liquidity*. This measure represents a company's ability to generate quick cash in order to respond to immediate growth opportunities, market challenges, competitive pressure, emergencies, and so on. Some large businesses are very sensitive to protecting working capital, some are less so. However, most senior executives will appreciate any product, service, or program that helps to generate more liquidity, and most will shy away from anything that is out of the ordinary in regard to liquidity. There are some ways to positively address working capital requirements:

- Provide payment terms that are longer or more friendly than normal, such as 60 days same as cash, pay on use, etc.
- Show how your product or service will result in quicker turns of their inventory, which provides a faster cash to cash cycle.
- Show how your product or service will result in less obsolete or slow moving inventory.

Of course, each of these options have pros and cons for the small business. Typically, small businesses are more sensitive to working capital requirements than a large business might be. Therefore, their opportunities may be limited in this way.

Total Delivered Costs

This measures the total actual costs to procure materials, manufacture the product, and ship and deliver the company's products to their customer. These costs typically make up at least half of the costs in the company. Obviously this has a major affect on bottom line profits, competitiveness, and the like. Therefore, senior management are typically very sensitive to any type of product or service that might increase costs and they are very receptive to any program that will reduce costs. Here are a couple of things to look out for:

- Management has usually been pitched a thousand times about some program or approach that will reduce costs. They will be very skeptical if the small business does not provide specific details of how this will be accomplished.

- Small business managers are notorious for their lack of understanding of the complexities of the large company's supply chain. As a result, they often fail to adequately understand or address key supply chain costs. Make sure to do your homework in this area.

Speed to Market

This measure addresses the company's ability to bring a new product to market in a timely and effective manner. Well run companies are typically very good at bringing new products to market. Along with new product effectiveness, companies measure the time it takes to bring a product to market from the time of concept to the time of product launch. This measure is a good indicator of the company's ability to execute once a decision has been made. Why does this matter to the small business? If the concept/product can be brought to market very quickly, it will typically get a better reception than a product that will take a long time to bring to market. Large companies clearly understand the importance of beating their competition to the marketplace and will be more likely to support a concept that accomplishes this.

Effectiveness of New Products

This measure is getting more and more traction among large businesses today. To my knowledge there is not a universally accepted name for this measure. However, most large companies have some way to define how well a new product met its original expectations. The reason this measure is so popular right now is because of the number of dismal failures companies have had among their new products. It is very common for a new product to come in at about half of its original projections. How does this occur? First there is a lot of pressure to launch effective new products for obvious reasons. Second, brand managers get a lot of positive strokes when they develop a concept and then launch that concept successfully. Third, in my opinion, marketing people are generally overly optimistic by nature and they are also very good at selling their ideas. Bottom line, a lot of new products come in with sales much lower than originally projected. The consequence of this is that costs are typically higher than projected, revenues are lower than projected, and overall profits are disappointing.

With this as background, it is no wonder that many senior managers have become somewhat jaded about overly optimistic numbers, thus they have devised a way to measure performance against original projections. So why does this matter to the small business manager? Like brand managers, small business partners are also notorious for over-projecting and under-delivering. Consequently, their numbers are seldom believed. It is very important for the small business manager to clearly address this concern and to make sure that projections are realistic and can be backed up with reliable analysis and data.

Quality

These days, a demand for quality is pretty well a given in any large corporation. As mentioned previously, large companies simply cannot afford to produce a substandard product. They typically have a host of measures and programs to continuously improve quality as well as operating efficiencies. You will hear of programs like Total Quality Management, Six Sigma, Lean Thinking, and the like. The small business may hear words like "Black Belt," "Kaisan Events," "Kanban," 5S, and so on. Some large corporations are very zealous about these programs to the point that small businesses are not even considered if they do not understand and support them. Therefore, it is essential for the small company to do their homework and be prepared to address concerns in this area, particularly if the small company is going to produce a product for the large business and will therefore need to strongly interact with the operations side of the business.

We began this chapter by asking if it would really make a difference to understand how large companies think and operate. Hopefully, we have made it clear that we think it is a major element negotiating a successful partnership. The more we understand about our customer, the more we can work to proactively address concerns and issues that may come up. In addition, the more we understand the way large companies think, the better we can work to present our product or service in a manner that will be accepted by the decision makers. Perhaps another key point not mentioned is one of confidence. The more we can speak the language, the more confident we will be in our presentation. At the end of the day, there is no better sales tool than confidence.

Chapter 5

Do Your Homework: Understanding Yourself and Your Partner

In Chapter 4 we discussed the importance of understanding the way large companies work in a general sense. In this chapter, we move our discussion to developing a clear understanding about your own company: what you have to offer and how that may or may not be a good fit with your potential partner.

You may wonder why we have included this chapter. Why not move right to Chapter 6 where we discuss ways to make the sale. The answer is really quite simple: By doing your homework and taking time up front to fully understand your own business and the business of your potential partners, you can save yourself much frustration and lost time. Like anything else, the more you know—about yourself and your potential partner—the more likely you are to succeed.

Consider This Scenario

XYZ company has been in business for approximately five years. Their product line-up consists of premium hair care and body products sold mainly to and through upscale resorts and spas and various high-end hair salons throughout the country. Customers love the products, and resort and spa owners love the high margins the products seem to generate.

The owners of the company are a husband and wife team, Bob and Emma. Bob is a chemical engineer who develops all the formulas and runs the operations side of the business. Emma is responsible for sales and marketing. Emma is an attractive, fun-loving person who makes friends everywhere she goes. Over the years, she has built a very loyal customer base. Bob and Emma pride themselves on providing high-quality products and terrific customer service. The business provides them with a great income and a comfortable lifestyle. However, they often wonder what it would take to move their business to the next level via a partnership with a larger company.

Now let's stop and consider what you might do with this company:

- Should you try to take it to the next level? What are the pros and cons of such a move? How would you take this next step?
- What type of company might be interested in the products this company produces? Who would you contact? What would you say to them?
- Do you really understand what you are selling? Do you know what it is worth?
- Do you have a timetable?

Now consider the questions a potential buyer/partner will have:

- Are they selling or licensing the formula?
- Are they selling or licensing the brand?
- Are they willing to give up their customer base?
- Are they selling their ability to service the customer or make a quality product?
- Do they want to sell the entire business?
- Do they want to stay in management?
- If they sell or merge, what happens to their employees?
- If they sell out completely, will the customers follow the product or Emma?
- Are they willing to sign a non-compete agreement? How many years?
- How much money do they need to make the deal work?
- Are they willing to let the larger company fulfill the orders?
- Do they want to continue making the product as a supplier to the large company?

Suppose that you are a manager at a large company, you love Bob and Emma's products, and you are interested in a potential partnership. Yet Bob and Emma have never really given any thought to the questions above. They simply throw out the idea of some type of relationship without really thinking through the particulars. Obviously, it would be impossible to move to the next step. In our experience, smaller businesses are notorious for making this very mistake. They really don't consider the questions a large business will ask, nor do they really analyze what they bring to the table in the potential partnership. Consequently, both parties become confused and frustrated, and unfortunately, many deals are lost in the process.

Know Yourself

Before you even start to think about approaching a potential partner you really need to understand your own company first. You may think you already know yourself pretty well, and in many ways you probably do. But have you considered your business from the standpoint of a potential partner?

Let's consider six basic questions the smaller business needs to consider.

What Are My Company's Strengths and How Might They Be Attractive to a Larger Company?

In the case of Bob and Emma's company, what to them is a strength may, in fact, not mean very much to their larger counterpart. For example, if they are going to pitch their company to a large consumer goods company, Emma's personal relationships with her customers may not mean very much because the large business is more likely to rely on mass media advertising. Additionally, they may not care very much about Bob's great quality control or order fulfillment because they have their own manufacturing and fulfillment facilities. On the other hand, XYZ's brand and the fact that it is sold exclusively in resorts and spas may be something the consumer goods company can leverage.

The story could be completely reversed with a different partner, though. If the partner is a direct competitor who has been having sales and fulfillment problems, they may be very attracted to Emma's sales capabilities and Bob's fulfillment expertise. The bottom line here is that indentifying your company's strengths compared to the potential partner's needs can make all of the difference in what you emphasize in your negotiations.

What Are Our Weaknesses and How Might They Be a Barrier to Making a Deal with a Larger Company?

The better we understand and acknowledge our weaknesses, the better we can work to proactively address them through a potential partnership. A key question to ask now is, "Why can't we grow our business without the partnership?" The answer may reveal some important insights:

- The business is cash poor.
- We really don't know how to sell to large customers.
- We don't have the management expertise or the energy.
- We don't have the expertise to "scale up" in the event of large volumes.
- Our ownership and management structure is not conducive to running a large business.
- We don't have adequate resources to protect our intellectual property.

As you come to understand and acknowledge your weaknesses, you can then take steps to either correct the weakness or, in the case of a partnership, you may be better able to consider what type of partnership would be most beneficial and successful. Such awareness will enable you to find a partner that is strong where you are weak, thereby creating a real win/win situation.

Too often, small companies approach a large company before they really know what they are trying to sell. Consequently, it feels like an attempt to throw something against the wall and see what sticks. When this happens, it rarely goes well. It is important to have addressed this question *before* contacting the large company. Imagine your frustration if you were a manager at a large business with genuine interest in a smaller company, and your potential partner hadn't considered what it was, exactly, they want to sell. If you don't know what kind of partnership you want, how will your potential partners?

Take a moment and consider what type of arrangement you want to form. Think about the following in terms of what you are selling to the larger company. What are we trying to sell to the larger company?

- A license
- A partnership
- A supplier relationship
- The entire business
- Some of the products
- All of the products
- Intellectual property
- Manufacturing capability

The manager at the large company may have a specific idea of how you can partner with them, but it is likely that they are waiting for you to say what you want. If all you need is a license or a supplier relationship, then asking for it straight out is a good move and a good way to not waste each other's time. In some cases, you might be willing to consider several options. Perhaps you are okay with just supplying your products to the larger company, but you would rather have them buy your company. If that is the case, then you can bring up a couple options as you investigate possibilities with them.

How Much Control Are We Willing to Give Up in a Partnership?

A major concern for many small businesses is one of control. For example, Bob and Emma may like running their own business. They may have a lot of emotion tied to their products, the packaging, the formula, and so on. Additionally, they may feel a strong attachment and responsibility to the employees of the business. Therefore, this is more than a financial decision for them. It can even feel like they are selling some of their children.

Depending on the situation, this can be a deal breaker. Large companies typically want as much control as they can get. Therefore, it is important to consider this issue before the negotiations begin. The more carefully you address this before approaching a partner, the better prepared you will be during the negotiation.

Let's look at a situation from an acquisition I am familiar with. The smaller company was offered a huge sum of money by a large company. The two partners had to think long and hard about the purchase because there was a culture in their company that was anti-large company and in particular the large company that was buying them. After a while the offer became too good to pass up. They decided to sell the company, and they gave up their control to the larger company. Things went well for the first few years, but the culture of the large company started to affect how the two original partners started treating each other. The politics of the larger company got to them, and one of the partners was eventually forced out of the company altogether. Two best friends ended up not liking each other anymore. In their case, there was a significant amount of regret about giving up control of their business.

In another situation, the owner of a company was ready to retire. He didn't want control of the company, because he wanted to move on with his life and reap the rewards of building a good company. In his case, selling the company made a lot of sense, and his only desire in sticking around for a few years was to make the transition easier. As it turned out, he only needed to be there for two years and then he felt fine in moving on.

As you can see from these two stories, giving up control meant different things to different owners. If you want to remain in the business and run your business while the larger company has control, you have to expect changes. If you feel an obligation to your company to keep things as they are, then you need to negotiate a partnership where you retain control of your company. Deciding what you want first is very important.

Do We Really Understand What Our Business/Products Are Worth?

This book is not about business valuation. However, determining your company's value is an important consideration before you approach a large business about a potential partnership. All too often, small businesses significantly under- or over-value their products or company. Consequently, they let emotions and lack of data get in the way of making a good deal. The more you know about the value of your offering, the better prepared you will be in a negotiation.

The bottom line for the value of any company is that it is what someone is willing to pay for it. With that in mind you can take a look at other companies that are similar to yours and see what they have sold for. Realize that this is only a ballpark estimate, because no two companies and no two deals are exactly the same, but it might help you begin to get an idea of worth. Another option is to take a close look at what it would cost you to buy what your company does. Over five or ten years, how much would you have to spend?

We are aware of a recent situation in which a small business owner was approached by a larger business in regard to selling part of the business. They offered one million dollars on the spot. In the small business owner's mind, a million dollars was a lot of money, so he took the offer without doing any homework. After all, he paid a lot less for it and he still had most of his business remaining. Imagine his surprise when only six months later, the company turned around and sold it to an even larger company for approximately 10 times as much.

A more typical scenario is one where the small company over-values their property and therefore can never get past first base as a consequence. A lot of anxiety can be saved by bringing in an outside expert to help with the valuation prior to any contact with the potential partner.

Investment banks that take companies to the public markets must calculate valuations all the time. Sometimes you can work with people from these companies or people who are retired from these companies to help you find a value for your company. Another good source for help in valuing your company is to talk with investors. See what they would value your company at. Sometimes seeking values from multiple sources and then averaging them can help you to come to a good idea of your company's value.

If the Company Has Multiple Owners, How Will We Meet the Needs of Each Person in This Deal? Do We Understand Each Person's Real Wants and Needs?

We have been amazed over the years by how many good deals failed due to the behavior of one or more of the owners. Typically this happens when one of the owners charges ahead with the negotiations without considering the needs—or power—of the other owners. What may seem like a perfectly good idea to the originating owner may not seem so great to the others. Additionally, personal egos often get in the way. Some owners may kill the deal simply because their opinions were not considered. Others may kill the deal because they have other motivations for the business. It is important to make sure that all key stakeholders' needs and feelings are considered—and conflicts resolved—before approaching any negotiation.

There is no magic answer to resolving internal conflict in preparation for a partnership. The best thing you can do is to have everyone involved be honest about what their individual objectives in the business are and work together to ensure that all of them are addressed. If you can't come to a workable solution, you might want to consider either buying some of the owners out or just putting the partnership search on hold until all parties agree.

In the end, the answers to these and many other questions can mean the difference between a successful and fruitful partnership and a long, drawn out process that ultimately leads to frustration and failure.

Know Your Potential Partner

While you are spending time getting to know yourself from a potential partner's point of view, it is also important to do your homework in regard to your potential partners. There are some questions you should be prepared to answer.

Do you have a list of potential partners? Depending on your industry, you may have only a couple large businesses that you can approach, or there may be dozens. It is always best to have options, so two or more potential partners is good.

Why would they be interested in working with you? What do you bring to their table? You should come up with a list of benefits you offer them. The more you know about them, the better you will be able to prepare this list.

On a scale of 1 to 10 how well do you know each of the potential partners in the following areas:

- What is their financial position?
- Are they currently in the same market as you?
- Would they see you, or your products, as significant competitors?
- Have they entered into partnership agreements in the past? How did those work out? Win/win, win/lose, lose/lose?
- What is the "management style" of the company? Is it a fit with your "style"?
- Would your product/company be considered a "strategic" fit with the potential partner or simply a "line extension" or cost saving offering?
- Do you know their corporate strategy? Where would you fit in their objectives, goals, and strategies?
- Do they have expertise in the market you currently sell in?

- Would they bring your product/company into a completely unknown market to them? To you?
- Do you know people in the company you can contact? If so, what level of management are they?
- Do they have a prescribed method of approaching other companies regarding partnerships/products?

Financial Position

Strong finances are important in a partnership, especially where there is the need for significant expansion. If you know that the partnership will need a lot of cash, and you are looking to your partner to provide that cash, take a hard look at the company's financial position.

In Your Market

If they are in your market already, partnering with your company might help them increase their market share. Companies that are already in your market may be prime candidates for partnerships. Even if they are not currently in your market, they may be interested in it. The only way to know is to ask.

Competitors

Like the item above, competitors many times make good partners because they already understand the market. Be careful, however, because sometimes a good way to get rid of a competitor is to buy them and then kill their products.

Track Record

Check out their past. If they have partnered with companies before, see how things went. Some companies are good at partnering, and some are not.

Management Style

Management style is primarily a compatibility check. If your styles match, you can have a great partnership. If they don't, you may have some work to do to get things to run smoothly.

Strategy Versus Extension

Strategic partnerships are often the most valuable for both parties. If you can find a good strategic fit with a company, you have the potential for building a good partnership. Product extensions and cost savings are good but maybe not as valuable.

Goals and Strategies

It is very helpful if you know what the potential partner's goals are and how your company might fit. Learning what they want can help you get what you want. See if you can find out what their objectives, strategies, and goals are.

Expertise

More than money, sometimes knowing the market can have huge value. Understanding your market will be of great benefit to you even if you think you already know it. They may have years of experience and contacts that will be very valuable in a partnership.

New Markets

Finding new markets either by region or category can be very valuable in a partner. For example, if you only sell in the United States, and they are strong in Europe but are also expanding in Asia, you could double or triple your sales.

Know People

It is always nice to do business with people you know. It helps to give you some background in the business. However, it only helps if the people you know have some relation to the part of the company you will be working with or in their management.

Proscribed Approach

Many larger companies handle partnerships in specific ways. It is always a good idea to find out if the company you want to partner with deals with partners in a way that is compatible with you and your company. You can also get more information from them and other partners if they always do partnerships in the same way.

In the initial stages of discovery, the larger the list of potential partners, the better. Hopefully, as you seek to answer the questions outlined here, you will then be able to narrow the list down to three or four solid candidates. When that is done, you are ready to move to the next phase.

The Seven Key Components of Any Large Business

As you analyze yourself and your potential partner, it is usually helpful to look at your business and the business of your potential partner from a business process point of view.

What Is a Business Work Process?

Almost all large and even small businesses can be divided into seven main areas called work processes. Simply stated, it is the way we do our work. Understanding how these processes relate to how things get done in a large business will help you as you talk with them about a partnership, because you will better see how your company can fit within their processes.

- Determine and communicate the objective
- Innovate
- Generate demand
- Satisfy demand
- Analyze results
- Manage and adjust
- Organizational and technical capability

The Operational Results, Inc. consulting company has created the process model in Figure 5.1 to depict the way these work processes function together in growing a company.

To understand the model, let's look again at Bob and Emma's business. In the beginning they had to have some sort of business objective and they needed to communicate that objective to each other and other key stakeholders. Then they had to have a product or an idea—they had to *innovate*. Bob developed a formula for a product, together they developed packaging, and so on. Then it was Emma's turn. Someone had to get out there and sell the product—they had to *generate demand*. As soon as Emma started generating demand, it was up to Bob to determine how to produce the product, take orders, and the like. He had to *satisfy demand*.

After that they needed to conduct an analysis to determine whether they were making money, satisfying their customers, and properly motivating their employees—they had to *analyze the impact*. Based on their findings they then needed to make appropriate adjustments—they needed to *manage* the business. Of course the glue that holds it all together is the *organizational* (human) and *technical* (systems, machinery, equipment) capability of the business.

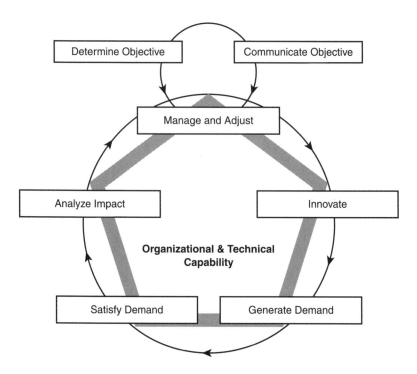

Figure 5.1 *This shows the basic matrix of the work process. Copyright – Operational Results, Inc. All rights reserved.*

From day to day, week to week, and month to month, the cycle continues. In order to grow, they must clearly articulate their objectives, they must keep innovating, keep generating demand, keep satisfying demand, continue analyzing results, and keep making appropriate adjustments. And, of course, they must continue to invest in organizational and technical capability. The better Bob and Emma perform each of the key work processes, the more their business will grow and prosper.

This core work process model has been used to help both large and small businesses understand their core competencies and their core weaknesses. Consider your own business: Do you know where your own business would stand against each section of this model? Now ask yourself, do you know where your potential partner would stand in each section?

As you analyze your own business, look at each section and try to determine your competitive advantages and your competitive weaknesses. Are you good at innovating, but not so good at generating demand? Do you innovate and generate demand, but then do a poor job of satisfying demand? Perhaps you feel you do a pretty good job at the first three areas, only to find out that you aren't really making any money. Do you clearly articulate your objectives?

Do you continue to invest in organizational and technical capability? And what about your potential partners? Where are they particularly strong or weak?

Answering these questions for yourself and your potential partner will help you determine whether you have a potential fit with your partner. Some key questions to ask are:

- Do we complement their core competencies?
- Do we increase competency in some area where they are weak?
- Do they bring competency in an area where we are weak?
- Are our strengths and their strengths the same such that we don't bring very much to the partnership?

Let's look at some examples.

If you were working on a partnership with Apple Computers, what could you bring to the partnership? What would they likely respect the most? Where are they particularly strong/weak?

Most people would say that Apple is particularly good at innovation. Therefore, if you were bringing a new product to Apple, it would likely have to be very good to succeed. You would know that it would be scrutinized by the very best, and they would be reluctant to even look at any potential product that might conflict with a product currently under development. Bottom line, it would likely be a very tough sell. However, if your product is really, really good, you would have some of the very best engineering and product development people in your camp.

What about Toyota? Like Apple, Toyota is really good at a lot of things. However, they are particularly good at satisfying demand. Therefore, if your key strength is in order fulfillment, you likely won't make much progress. They already consider themselves very good in that way. On the other hand, if you have a great, high-quality product for the automotive business, but you are lousy at order fulfillment, you may be on to a good partnership.

What if you were working on a partnership with The Home Depot? It is well understood that they are very good at controlling costs and satisfying demand; that is the way they have grown their business. They provide great product assortment at a lower price than most other hardware stores. Therefore, they would likely be interested in high-quality products at affordable prices and not so interested in new and improved mousetraps.

There is no right or wrong answer. By analyzing each of the core work processes of yourself and your potential partner, you will come to understand more completely where you can have a win/win opportunity. Some companies use the following model to help them analyze this fit. Of course, it is important to have more than just a gut feeling as to your strengths and weaknesses or the strengths and weaknesses of your partner. The more homework you do, the more valuable the exercise.

Figure 5.2
Viewing the strengths together helps to identify synergy.

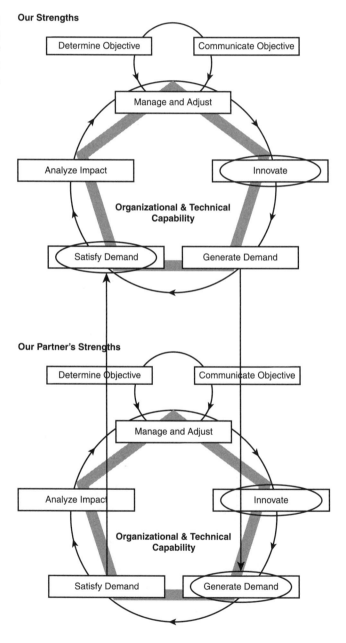

Typically, the best fit occurs when partners are at polar opposites or when they are directly on top of each other in the model.

As you work to analyze your own business and the business of your potential partner, let's look at some important considerations in each area.

Determine and Communicate the Objective

This area describes the way a company develops its objectives and the way it communicates its objectives to its shareholders, customers, and employees. Many companies refer to this as their annual strategic planning and business planning work process. Most publicly held corporations go to great lengths to develop and communicate their business strategies. With each passing year, strategic planning processes become more and more robust. The best companies are very careful to develop well-thought-through strategies and then to stick with the strategy. Therefore, it is important that the small business counterpart understands how and where they support their large business partner's strategy. If they have a product or service that complements the strategy in some way, they have a good possibility of a partnership. On the other hand, if their product or service runs counter to the current strategy, then it will likely be a tough sell. Consequently, the more you know about your large business counterpart's strategy and business plan, the more you will be able to address their key concerns.

Innovation

As you think about your own business and the business of your potential partner, where do you each fall in regard to innovation? Do you consider innovation a core competency of your business or your potential partner's business? As you think about your products or services, would you say they are truly innovative (or rather more efficient or less costly)? Are you bringing in a completely new product offering or simply a line extension? What makes your product unique? Do you have a patented or copyrighted product? Will your product be hard to duplicate? Does your product or service bring a serious competitive advantage to your partner in some way? Do you have strong innovation work processes? Can you bring a new product to market quickly and efficiently?

If the answers to the questions above are mostly yes, then you may want to look for a partner that is looking for a new product, rather than line extensions, cost savings, and the like. As you consider which way to go, recognize that you basically have two different options: 1) look for a partner who is very good at innovation and who may be able to take your product to market quickly; or 2) look for a partner who is perhaps not very good at innovation, but is very good at generating demand and satisfying demand. Perhaps you could find someone who desperately needs a new product and who would put significant efforts behind its growth. As you determine which road to follow, you will then know how to proceed in regard to making the first contact.

As you prepare to contact the company's marketing or product development group, make sure you understand how the company actually develops and markets new products. What processes or steps do they follow when developing a new product? How much time do they take? What is their current process for approving a new product? Most large companies follow a *stage-gate* process in developing new products. Each "stage" has a defined set of criteria that must be met before the concept/product can pass through the "gate" to the next stage. For most large companies, the stage-gate process is rigorous and inviolate. Additionally, the larger the impact, the more people will be involved in the approval process. Consequently, the process can seem very bureaucratic and time consuming to the smaller business partner. The more you understand about stage-gate product development processes, the more you will be able to work with your large business counterpart to be able to move your product through the steps and into the marketplace.

What if you are selling an idea rather than a product or service? First, it must be said that ideas are a tough sell to most large corporations; they generally have lots of ideas already. Therefore, they tend to put much less value on ideas and much more value on an actual tangible products or services. Consequently, it is usually much more advantageous to convert the idea to an actual product or service before approaching the larger corporation.

With that said, if you do believe you have a truly great idea and you can't wait to show it to the potential partner, make sure you follow the steps to protect your intellectual property as we outlined in Chapter 3 before contacting the partner. It is very difficult to prove an idea was yours first if you have no copyrights, non-disclosure agreements, and the like.

Generate Demand

As mentioned in Chapter 4, most large companies spend inordinate amounts of effort tracking volume and revenue growth. Second only to profit, these are the most highly monitored measures. Therefore, before approaching a potential partner, it is important to consider exactly how you expect them to sell or market your product or service. And if you are going to sell their products or services, it is just as important that you have considered exactly how you are going to market and sell their items.

Here are some very important questions you will need to be able to answer to their satisfaction:

- How will the product or service be priced at each stage of the supply chain from consumer back to the distributor, manufacturer, and so on?
- What profit margin can your large business counterpart expect to gain through the sale of these products?
- Is this margin better or worse than most of the products the large business sells?
- How will this margin be protected over time?
- What volume of sales do you believe the product can generate in its first six months, first year, first two years? How did you arrive at those projections? (You need to have solid, believable answers to this question.)
- How will this product complement or cannibalize current product offerings? (Again, you will need good data on this.)
- What will this do for us in regard to market share?
- How much effort will this product take to sell? Does it require a lot of personal selling and extra training for our sales people? What's in it for the sales people? Why would they want to sell this product?
- What are your recommendations on the most effective method of selling this product? Direct sales? Mass media advertising? Internet sales?
- Does it require a completely new market channel or does it fit current market channels?
- How well does this fit with the current marketing and sales approach? Same/different sales territories? Same/different commission structures?
- How will orders for this product or service be satisfied? How will it affect the current customer service objectives?
- What assurance can you give in regard to product quality? How do we know the customer will be excited about this product today and in the future?

As you prepare to answer these questions, recognize that it is of utmost importance that you have done your homework and that your answers are data based and well considered. Good answers to these questions almost always mean the difference between success and failure. Remember that senior management hear pitches all the time, both internally and externally. They will immediately recognize those who have done their homework and those who have not. Those who have not done their homework seldom get a second chance. Additionally, it is typically better to be slightly conservative rather than overly optimistic.

It is also important to avoid pitching a product or service that will require serious changes to the current sales approach (sales method, territory, commission structure, etc.). These seldom find success at the end of the day. Recognize that large corporations are like large ships; it is hard for them to change course. Unless your product offering and sales approach is specifically named in the corporate strategy, it is usually better to find another partner. It is just too hard and too time consuming to make it work.

Satisfy Demand

Now let's consider the *satisfy demand* set of work processes. In the partnership, who will be expected to satisfy the demand? In other words, who will make the product, provide the service, ensure product quality, handle customer orders, manage inventories, and so on. After determining who is responsible for this work, the next key question is how it will be accomplished.

While not typically as critical as generating demand when making that first pitch to your potential partner, the ability to satisfy demand will surely be a key component in meeting expectations and in keeping the partnership viable and healthy over the long haul. Therefore, it is very important that these processes be considered carefully. Let's start with the first question: Who will be responsible for satisfying demand?

As you consider this, please recognize that one mistake a lot of small companies make is underestimating the difference in volume between their business and the larger business. Consequently, they typically underestimate the amount of organizational and technical capability they will need to keep up with the growth. They tend to hold on to the notion that they can handle the fulfillment requirements necessary to support their large business counterpart, even when they have no technical right to have that notion.

Additionally, small businesses tend to have a mentality that they will adjust their equipment to match demand as it happens rather than before it happens. They tend to say, "A million cases would be a nice problem to have. I'll deal with it when it gets here." What they don't realize is that it typically takes anywhere from 12 to 18 months to scale up to meet a national launch. All too often, they "shoot themselves in the foot" before they even get started. When they can't keep up with demand, they lose important momentum just when they need it the most, and they lose credibility with their partner, with the sales team, with the customer, and with the end consumer. Most of the time, this credibility cannot be regained.

With this in mind, we recommend extreme caution before committing to handle all of the production and order fulfillment responsibilities for your large business counterpart. Ask yourself, do you really believe the demand projections you gave to your partner? What if they beat it by double? Would you be able to handle the growth? Do you have the financial resources and organizational and technical capability to stay ahead of the curve? If the answers to any of these questions are no, then you must step back and reconsider before committing to the arrangement. Another good question to ask yourself is why you want to handle the production and fulfillment. If the answer is one of keeping control or reluctance to give up "your baby," then you should reconsider. If, on the other hand, the answer is that it is a critical component of getting the deal or it is already one of your core competencies, then you will likely want to keep control of the fulfillment process.

Assuming you have determined that you will be doing the fulfillment, here are some key questions you will need to answer when meeting with your large business counterpart:

- How much capacity do you already have?
- How is that capacity allocated?
- Without a capital expenditure, how much excess capacity do you have?
- How much surge potential do you have?
- Based on the current set of volume projections, when will you need to invest in new human or technical capability?
- How much time will it take to double your current capacity? Triple it?
- Do you have outside contract suppliers you can use if you cannot keep up with demand?
- How will you warehouse and transport the product line?
- What are the lead time requirements you will require to meet customer orders?
- How will you handle customer orders, complaints, and so on?
- How will your fulfillment process interface with your partner's fulfillment process in order to appear seamless to the customer?
- Do you have the financial resources to keep up with inventory and equipment requirements?

- How much inventory (in days of forward coverage) will you keep on hand?
- How will you continue to drive costs down?
- How will you ensure product quality?
- How will you ensure employee safety?
- What are your work processes relative to production planning, scheduling, and procurement?

As you consider the answers to these questions for your own business, it is also important to try to understand as much as you can about your partner's fulfillment processes. See if you can answer the same questions about your partner. The more you know about them, the better you will be able to address their key concerns. For example, perhaps they are completely out of capacity and warehouse space. If that is the case, you may find an even greater opportunity in offering to take on more of their product fulfillment processes. On the other hand, if they have excess capacity or warehouse space, it may be advantageous to both parties to allow them to do the fulfillment.

As mentioned in Chapter 4, take some time to analyze potential concerns from different functions in the large business. You may find that you have allies on one hand and enemies on the other. For example, if the large business' operations department has been delivering less than great customer service, you may have an ally in sales and marketing for allowing your business to do the fulfillment. Therefore, you may want to pitch sales and marketing on the idea before approaching operations. However, you will need to recognize that your proposal may cause operations to have to reduce staff or shut down lines, something they usually are not too keen on. Therefore, be prepared for the torpedo coming from operations.

The more you understand about your own capability and the capability of your potential partner, the more effective you will be in addressing their key concerns.

Analyze the Impact

There is usually a significant difference between the amount of effort small businesses and large businesses expend to analyze business results. Consider financial reporting. The small business may have an outside accounting firm that periodically reviews their books and prepares yearly tax returns. On the other hand, the large business usually has large staffs of internal accountants who spend every day analyzing where they are making money, where they are losing money, and so on. Additionally, they often have very expensive big-six accounting firms reviewing their records and making recommendations.

This same difference in emphasis can be seen in most of the other operating measures we discussed in Chapter 4. It's not that small businesses don't measure these things, it's just that they don't have the same rigor and scope of measurements. Large businesses have multiple layers of management, multiple divisions, more stakeholders, etc. Consequently, they have to have rigorous, well-defined metrics in order to stay in control.

So how does this affect the small business owner? If you are looking for a significant partnership with your large business counterpart, you will not only need to speak their language, you also need to present your own business in that language. For example, you will need to have analyzed and come prepared to discuss your business using each of the key measures we discussed in Chapter 4: ROIC, revenue, volume, market share, customer service, total delivered costs, working capital, speed to market, and new product effectiveness. Additionally, the more you know about their performance against each of these key measures, the better you will be able to address their key concerns and opportunities.

Finally, as mentioned in Chapter 4, you will need to come prepared to show how your proposal positively impacts each of the key measures above. If it does not positively impact one area or another, you will need to show them how the other measures clearly offset the loss. If your proposal does not positively impact most of the key measures above, it will likely not make it very far. These measures are critically important for most large businesses. Failure to adequately address them will typically lead to failure. On the other hand, if you positively address each of the key metrics and your numbers are believable, you will almost always win the deal.

Manage and Adjust

It is usually very difficult for a small business owner to rate their own management style and capability, yet this area is often a key component in sealing a long term deal with a large business counterpart. Let's go back to Bob and Emma's business. Obviously, Bob and Emma have done a lot of things right. Therefore, they must be good managers, right? It depends. In the context of a small business they are probably good managers. In the context of a large business, however, it's not so clear. How successful would they be as managers if the business were 10 times larger? What about 100 times larger? Have they demonstrated an ability to hire and mentor other managers? Do they have a good grasp of strategic planning, organizational behavior, shareholder relations, financial reporting, succession planning, and so on? Like many small business owners, Bob and Emma may have built the business by being very involved in every aspect of the business. All key decisions may flow through them, and they may not even have anyone on staff with serious management experience. If this is the case, it may be very hard to convince their large business counterpart that they are ready to handle significant growth or interact in the board room. On the other hand, if Bob and Emma have developed a solid team of managers around them, they demonstrate good delegation capability, and they can speak the language of the boardroom, Bob and Emma will be more likely to be seen as peers.

Does it matter? Of course each situation has its own set of circumstances. If the small business is simply selling out or selling its intellectual property, it probably doesn't matter that much; the acquiring company will not really consider it a factor. However, in just about every other relationship, it will matter a lot. Most large businesses are reluctant to enter into a long term arrangement of any significance without first having confidence in the management team. After all, would you want to link your company with a company that relied on one person to make all of the critical decisions? What if the person got sick, got ran over by a bus, or decided to just quit? Obviously, it would be a real problem. Therefore, almost all large companies do some sort of assessment of the management team before entering into a long term relationship.

So how do you address the management question with your large business counterpart? The first step is to get unvarnished feedback from someone who regularly interacts with senior management at larger corporations. Ask someone you respect to spend a few days watching you in action, to spend a few days with various members of your management team, and then ask for specific (and confidential) feedback. Here are some questions you should ask them to address:

The Boss

- Does he/she clearly articulate the company vision, objectives, goals, and strategies?
- Would these items be considered strategic by their large business counterpart?
- Does he/she teach principles before practices?
- Does he/she delegate on a regular basis? Really delegate?
- How well does the boss mentor other employees?
- Does the boss maintain respect while treating subordinates with dignity and consideration?
- Does the boss manage by exception?
- How well does the boss manage his/her time?

- Does he/she have a clear set of measurements and expectations? How do these compare to large business measurements?
- Does he/she speak the language of a large corporation?
- What kind of people does the boss respect and promote? Yes men? Strong willed? People who speak their mind? Hard workers? Social and fun-loving people? Articulate? Good dressers? Highly educated? Poorly educated? College buddies? Experienced managers?
- Does he/she have a succession plan?
- What kind of management meetings does the boss have? How are they led and organized?
- Do people like to work for the boss? Why? Would they say if they didn't?
- Do people like to work at XYZ company? Do they see it as a long term place to work?

The Direct Reports

- Do they have other options beside XYZ company? Why have they stayed with XYZ company?
- Analyze their skill and experience in the area they are assigned to.
- Analyze their education level.
- How do they interact with the boss? Do they speak their mind?
- How well do they manage their direct reports?
- Are they motivated to take the business to the next level?
- Do they have the skills and knowledge to take the business to the next level?
- How would they stack up against their large business counterpart?
- Would they stay with XYZ in a merger with a larger company?
- Would the larger company want to keep this person?

You may say, "Hey, wait a minute here. I'm not trying to sell out; I'm just trying to create a partnership with the larger company. Why all of this analysis of my management style or the capability of my team?" The answer is simple: These questions will be on the mind of the larger company management team, even if they do not articulate it. As mentioned above, large companies are typically quite wary of doing business with a one-man-shop. And it is universally recognized that even mid-size businesses can be fundamentally a one-man-shop. Most large companies want to do business with a management team who will be around for the long haul, who can handle the growth, and who can speak the corporate language.

A few years ago, I had an acquaintance who owned a small aerospace and defense company. In the early years, the business had grown very rapidly. However, when I met the owner, the business had stopped growing and was starting to decline, and the owner was becoming increasingly frustrated by the lack of growth. Fortunately, within a few months, the owner received an offer of approximately $10 million; he sold out and retired. Not a bad story; $10 million is a lot of money for anyone. Yet, within a few years, the business was worth at least 10 times as much and was subsequently sold to a much larger aerospace and defense contractor.

So how did the company gain that much value in such a short period of time? The market or product line did not change all that much. The difference was in the management team. When my acquaintance owned the business, every decision had to go through him (by all accounts, every decision really meant *every decision*). Additionally, although the owner did have a management team, the team consisted of family and friends with little, if any, management experience. They were all dependent on the owner for their day-to-day living and consequently deferred to him. He didn't respect any of them as peers, and they didn't give him any reason to change his opinion. When the business was quite small, his style worked okay. However, at a certain point, he simply was not capable of being everywhere and doing everything. Consequently, the business stopped growing. Fortunately, the owner was wise enough to sell out while he still had a viable company. Unfortunately, he sold out for a fraction of the business' worth had it had a good management team.

So, what if you don't score very well in the previous assessment? What if your business looks a lot like the business above? How should you handle it? First, recognize that regardless of a partnership with a large business, your business will ultimately reach a plateau if you do not develop your management style and the capability of your team. Therefore, it is always in your best interest to take steps to build a strong team. Second, recognize that you can change direction before approaching your large business counterpart. Third, recognize that most senior managers understand the difficulty of developing and mentoring a management team. Therefore, if you acknowledge some weakness in this way, but show a willingness to make necessary changes, you will often find that senior managers are more than willing to help you. The worst thing to do is to be completely clueless about your management weaknesses and consequently fail to recognize any shortcomings in this area. Make no mistake, your large business counterpart will certainly recognize the oversight and will adjust the offer accordingly.

Organizational and Technical Capability

We have generally covered these topics in our previous discussion relative to satisfying demand or in managing the business. Therefore, we will not add a lot more to this section. The key point here is to show your large business counterpart that you can "scale up" with them. You will need to demonstrate that you have the technology or you know how to get it and that you have the human capability or you know how to get it. The more you address this up front, the better you will do. As mentioned above, you do not need to be perfect in this area. You just need to show awareness of your shortcomings and the motivation to make necessary changes.

Summarizing Your Homework

As you complete your analysis of your own business and the business of your potential partner, you will typically find a lot of areas you can improve on. Hopefully you will also find many areas of strength that can be emphasized. Based on this analysis, you should be able to prepare a good presentation that can be used to make your first contact. The more thorough you have been, the more attention you will typically receive. We suggest taking the time to formally document your findings in each of the core work process areas mentioned above. Then, as you meet with various potential partners, you can begin to add more meat to each section as needed. Eventually, when you are meeting with the senior management team of your large business counterpart, they will be quite impressed with your presentation. This often translates to achieving your goal. Perhaps even more importantly, by completing these analyses you will come to know more clearly what it is you are looking for in a partner and how to go about finding it.

Chapter 6

Making It Happen

Y ou've done your homework. You know what you want and you know what company you want to partner with. You've taken the time to learn about the company. You're ready to go make the deal. So how do you do it? That is what this chapter is all about. It's time to make it happen, and hopefully we can give you the tools you need to do it right.

Gatekeepers and Decision Makers

Unless you're well connected you will have to go through the gatekeepers before you can reach the decision makers. *Gatekeepers* are the people that large companies hire to sift through all the incoming offers to distinguish the good ones from the bad ones. Their job is to save time for higher level executives by culling out the people, companies, and propositions that are a waste of the company's time.

A *decision maker* is the person in a company that has the authority to make a deal with another company. They are usually higher level executives with extensive experience and high levels of trust within the company. They are the ones you want to talk with, but they are not always the ones you get to talk with. Often you have to go through several levels of management before you reach a true decision maker.

Your real goal is to get your ideas in front of a decision maker. To do that you will likely need to talk to a number of gatekeepers first. Rather than getting frustrated with the process, though, you must use it to your advantage. Gatekeepers play a vital role in any large company. If you play your cards right, you can have the gatekeeper pass your idea up the ladder while all of your competitors' ideas are given the boot.

Gatekeepers

Gatekeepers have a tough job. They only have the authority to reject deals; they don't have the authority to make them. In most companies there is no official title of gatekeeper. It is just a moniker that is applied by those outside the company. Gatekeepers are usually lower level managers or administrative assistants to higher level executives. They usually don't have the same insight into the business that the higher level executives do and because of that they are given a set of rules that they follow to determine which deals or business opportunities to pass along to the upper level folks and which ones to reject.

Even though the gatekeeper may not have the same level of business judgment that an upper level executive might have, they still know a lot about the company and how things work. Sometimes they may even know more than some of the upper level bosses. This is particularly true of administrative assistants.

If you want to reach someone who really can make a decision, you stand a much better chance of getting that person's attention if you first make an ally of the gatekeepers for that person. Read on for a few suggestions.

Getting Through (not Past) the Gatekeeper

Gatekeepers control the gate to the company, and they are there for a reason. You won't make any friends by trying to get around them. Even though they may not be decision makers, they are there because they have the ear of the decision makers. They are the filter the company uses to make sure higher level executives spend their time more effectively.

If you think of a gatekeeper as a filter, then you can see their value. People buy water filters in their homes because they want to drink filtered water. Sure, they can drink water straight from the tap but they prefer filtered water because filtering removes all of the impurities. The gatekeeper works in the same way with partnership proposals: They help to keep the bad ones out and let the good ones through. Working with them can be a big help in getting your partnership proposal greater visibility within the company.

I will often try to talk things through with a gatekeeper to get their opinion on a proposal. I remember one instance when I sent what I thought was an exciting and interesting proposal to a company. The gatekeeper seemed less than enthusiastic about my idea but he did show interest.

Rather than take no for my answer, I questioned him about why he thought it wouldn't fly. As we talked, I discovered that he actually liked the idea but didn't think he could sell it to the company as it was. We talked further through email about what the company might go for. I used his insight into the company to re-draft my proposal. We exchanged ideas for several weeks until one day he said he thought the proposal was ready. By developing a relationship with this gatekeeper, not only did we make a proposal that was better suited to the company, we also built his confidence and enthusiasm for the project. Ultimately our proposal was a success and we were able to make the partnership.

The point here is that gatekeepers can be your ally. If you stop looking at them as an obstacle and focus instead on developing a friendship with them, you might be surprised at what they can do to help you. They often have very good insight into the company. They know what the company is looking for and that information alone is very valuable.

As I said earlier, the gatekeeper is a filter. Working with them to take the impurities or problems out of your partnership ideas can lead to a more successful shot at getting a good deal. The trick is not to try to jump over them but to use them to filter your ideas. If you are used to drinking filtered water, you are not going to appreciate unfiltered water. If the company you want to partner with is used to getting filtered ideas, they are not going to like getting unfiltered ones. That is why they have a gatekeeper.

Sometimes you may run into a wall because the gatekeeper just doesn't like your idea. You may think that he or she just doesn't see the vision, and you may be right. However, you may more likely be wrong. If, after a lot of work and correspondence with the gatekeeper, you still find yourself at a dead end, you really only have two choices. One choice is to look for another partner; the other choice is to look for another gatekeeper. There is usually more than one gatekeeper for a business. Maybe one of the others will be more receptive.

Recently I talked with a friend of mine who runs one of the premier animation schools at one of the nation's largest universities. When he was first trying to get the school started he was part of the art department. Try as he might, he just couldn't get the funding for the expensive digital animation computers and systems he needed. The other art faculty consistently voted for more traditional expenditures. They just didn't have the same vision as he did.

One day he was talking to a friend from the engineering department. His friend said that his problem was not how to convince the other faculty in the art department to spend money on new computers; it was that his program was in the wrong department. The engineering department had all kinds of computers. So my friend went to the engineering department and told them his vision. They liked the idea and the animation program was moved from the art department to the engineering department, where it flourished and became one of the best in the country.

Your idea may be a good one but you might be approaching the wrong part of the company. You may even be approaching the wrong company. Instead of trying to convince an unyielding gatekeeper to let your idea through, your time might be better spent looking for another gatekeeper or looking for another company altogether.

Don't Ever Lie to Get Past a Gatekeeper

Lies are bad for business in any situation. Telling a lie to further your business opportunities will almost always come back in a negative way at some point in the future. Lying to a gatekeeper is one of the worst business decisions you can ever make. It is easy to think that the gatekeeper is holding you up from important business and if you could just get past him or her, you could talk to someone with greater knowledge that would see the true benefits of your partnership idea. Shading the truth just a little to get past the gatekeeper and talk to someone with real power might be awfully tempting. But it will likely end in disaster.

A gatekeeper's job is to pass on information to their managers. If you lie to them, that lie will be passed up to the managers that you want to talk to before you have a chance to talk with them. This will create a false expectation for when you do talk with them. You will then be faced with two tough decisions: lie to them again or admit that you lied before. Neither choice will help you. If you choose to lie again you will find that the lies will continue to mount and eventually you will be found out. If you admit that you lied, you will likely go no farther with the company. People do not like being lied to. When you lie to a gatekeeper you are lying to the company.

Be Friendly

One of the best things you can learn to do when it comes to building an alliance with a large company is to be friends with everyone you meet within that company. I am not talking about building false friendships for the mere purpose of gaining access to higher level people. What I mean is to go out of your way to befriend anyone and everyone you can that works for the company.

When you visit the company, greet everyone in an open and friendly manner. Take genuine interest in people and be sincere about it. This may sound simplistic, but you will be amazed at how it can quickly create a warm and pleasant atmosphere. In today's society people are either plugged in or hyperfocused on tasks. Finding someone who is pleasant and cheerful is a breath of fresh air.

I once worked with a person who had that ability to make friends on the spot. He was open and pleasant to everyone. He had no problem striking up a conversation with anyone, anywhere. If we were on a bus, he would be talking to someone riding with us. If we were at a restaurant, he would visit with the servers and sometimes even talk with the cooks. He was free with his compliments but never false. When we would walk into a meeting he would quickly get to know every person in the room. It usually took more time to get things done when I worked with him than other colleagues because much of our time was spent getting to know the people we met.

The interesting thing about him was that people remembered him. We often had people come up and say hello. Because he was so open, others were open with him in return. I would have to rate him as the most effective salesperson I ever had the chance to work with. His sales numbers were off the charts compared to other salespeople. He just had that ability to get people to tell him what they really needed and that opened the doors for him to find a way to help them. I know of a few highly motivated sales professionals who might have generated more overall sales, but none of them had as much repeat sales as he did.

Why do I bring up this person here in our discussion of gatekeepers? It is because you never know when a friendship will turn the opinion of a company. If all things are equal and you have no other advantage over your competition, the mere fact that everyone at the company likes you better than everyone else gives you a huge advantage.

Not everyone will feel comfortable being open and friendly. Some people are shy; some are just naturally more reserved. Some people may just not have very good people skills. If you are one of these people, you may find it difficult to reach out to others in an open and friendly way.

Everyone has their strengths and yours may not be making friends with everyone you meet. This doesn't mean that you shouldn't try to make friends; it just means that you should do it in your own way. Rather than trying to change your nature, you may find it helpful to hire someone who has great people skills and work together to make friends. As a rule it is always better to be genuine than try to put on a false front. Some people go about making friends in a quiet, unassuming way. The important thing is that the friendship is sincere and not false.

Do I Know You?

A wise person once told me when I was first starting my career that people tend to like to do business with people they know. In other words, if I wanted to work and prosper in the industry, I should get to know as many people as I could. Over the years I have found his advice to be very accurate.

It sometimes makes you wonder why, in the culinary capital of the world Paris, France, where the choices of restaurants are almost endless and the quality of the food is so high, that one of the busiest places to eat for American tourists is McDonald's. The reason is quite simple: People go to McDonald's in Paris because they know exactly what they are going to get. It isn't that the food is better; it is that the food is known. The same thing is true for business. Your service or product might be better but because it is an unknown, it gets passed over for a product that is better known.

If you want to become a partner with a large company, you have to get to know them and they have to get to know you. You get to know each other one person at a time. One of the first things you should do is to find out who you should get to know.

Finding the Right People

Not everyone in a company will be in a position to help you make a partnership. Some will be more helpful than others. While getting to know everyone you can at a company is important, you still need to understand what role each person might play in helping you to move your partnership idea forward. It does you no good to ask someone to do something that they have no ability or authority to accomplish. For example, you might make great friends with the head of a plant, but asking that person to approve a company-wide alliance with your company is out of their area of influence.

To better understand how each person fits into the overall puzzle, think of them in the following terms:

- Approver
- Decision maker
- Decision starter
- Influencer
- Good will

Each position on the list above serves an important role. Let's take a look at each one in more detail.

Approver

The *approver* is usually a high-level executive such as a vice president or above. They are the people who approve budgets and authorize deals between companies. They may not make the actual decision to partner with another company, although they have that authority. Their usual role is to approve the decisions made by lower level managers and authorize the budget for those decisions.

Approvers are those executives who have budgetary discretion and autonomy, meaning they are trusted to make decisions on budgets. Depending on the size of the company and the company's budgeting practices they may be the board of directors. They may be the company's president. They may be a senior level vice president.

The reason an approver is important is that they will be the last level of management you need to work with to get your partnership idea off the ground. They can also play a major role in how your idea is viewed by other people within the company. Companies as a whole look to the top level management for direction. If a top level manager likes an idea, it will likely get done. On a scale of important people to get to know, the approver has to be near the top.

Decision Maker

Another very important person to get to know is the *decision maker*. The main difference between a decision maker and the approver is that the decision maker is the one at the company that actually decides that the partnership should happen. They may not have the authority to make the deal happen, but they are the ones that decide the deal should happen and will present it to the rest of the company for approval to move forward.

In some instances, decision makers and approvers may be the same person. It is more likely, however, that they are different. The decision maker is usually the manager who will benefit the most from partnering with your company. They will be one of the most important people you meet in terms of achieving a partnership arrangement with the company.

Decision Starter

The primary difference between a decision starter and a decision maker is one of authority. A *decision starter* may well like the idea of a partnership and may actually be a huge champion for it within the company, but the decision starter has no real authority to make the partnership happen. The role played by the decision starter is to start the ball rolling within the company.

Sometimes it is difficult to tell decision starters from decision makers because decision starters often like to give the impression that they have more authority than they actually do. I've seen cases in which the decision starter claims to be able to get a deal to work in a company, only to find out later that they have no real authority. This can often lead to disappointment on the part of the small business owner, who has spent a significant amount of time working with the decision starter only to find out that there are several layers of management between them and a solid partnership deal.

As a general rule, approvers and decision makers are very few in number and usually very high up in management. Seldom will a plant manager, regional VP, or manager have that type of authority.

The decision starter does play a vital role in the process, but they are only the beginning. Never assume that the manager you are talking to actually has the authority to make a partnership happen unless they are at the very top of the company. Question the manager about who needs to approve the project and how the approval process works. Also question others who work at the company to see where the real power lies.

Influencer

An *influencer* is anyone in a company that can encourage or influence a positive reception of the partnership idea. Influencers can come from any part of the company. They can be high-level executives that work in a different division or they can be low-level employees that work directly with more influential managers. Influencers are located throughout the company and they can have a dramatic impact on your credibility with the company.

Influencers play the important role of endorsing you or your company. Managers at large companies usually want to avoid making unpopular (or uneducated) decisions. They often will seek out the opinions of others who may know a company firsthand. For example, a manager may ask in a meeting if anyone has had dealings with a certain company. If the answer is yes, the manager will likely want to know how things went. I serve on the board of a local organization that serves entrepreneurs in our area. There are a number of other people who serve on the board with me from both large and small companies. It is very common for a member of the board to reach out to the rest of us concerning someone they are thinking of doing business with just to see if anyone knows the person. I have seen a number of deals never get off the ground because someone on the board had a negative comment about the person in question. I have also seen scenarios in which a strong endorsement has resulted in greater opportunity for the person or company in question.

The point is that top level managers are people just like the rest of us, and they talk to others about what they are doing. If you can get a few positive endorsements, you stand a much better chance to move your partnership idea forward.

Good Will

Good will is a general positive feeling that people at a company have toward you and your company. Gaining good will is not so much an individual effort, so it doesn't involve a person like the other categories, but it can definitely work to your advantage. You gain good will by doing positive things that become known to people at a company. For example, I work with a group that sponsors an annual award program for new companies that are less than five years old. The award program honors new companies that have shown significant growth. Companies are graded based on revenue growth and job creation and ranked from best to worst. Those companies that rank the highest are honored at an annual event; they also receive significant local and regional press. The event attracts a lot of interest in the community—

including interest from many larger companies. Ranking high or at the top can help a new company achieve good will with a larger company because the executives see and often remember those companies.

Good will can come from business performance, like in the previous example, and it can also come from community involvement. Top level executives are often involved in community programs, and if they aren't, others at their company usually are. Serving in community programs as an individual or sponsoring community programs can help to increase good will for you and your company, which can then lead to a positive feeling with other companies that also serve in the community.

I remember getting a phone call from someone I had never heard of before. He introduced himself as the president of a large company that was in a totally unrelated industry. He asked me a few questions and then asked for a meeting. The final result was a partnership with the company developing an innovative new product. I later found out that someone who I served with in our local religious group was visiting with him and suggested he contact me because my company worked on products in an area that they were interested in moving into. I had gained good will by working in a group completely outside my business. Because others in the group respected me, they became advocates for me in their own companies.

Preparing for Your First Meeting

Contacting a large company and setting up that first meeting is your first real step to achieving a partnership. Before you make that call, however, there are a few things that you should do first to help prepare for a successful meeting.

- Research
- Networking
- Building recognition
- Being in the right place at the right time

Research

We've talked a lot about getting to know people and we have even talked a little about what types of people you should get to know and what roles they may play in helping you to get your partnership idea in front of the right people. This is all fine and good if you know who the right people are within a company. One thing that will help you to gain a much better chance of meeting and developing a relationship with the people who can help you the most is to do a little research before you approach the company.

Finding out who to talk to at a company is usually not too difficult. The top managers at a company often are listed on the company's website. If the company is a public company, there will be a list of top managers in the company's annual report. These two resources can go a long way toward giving you a list of people that you want to get to know.

Sometimes direct research is the best way to learn about a company. I remember one company that I wanted to approach, but I didn't know anyone at the company and I didn't know anyone that I could ask about the company, so I just called. When the receptionist answered I simply asked to be transferred to the person that was responsible for the type of deal that I wanted to make. In order for the receptionist to understand what I wanted, I had to explain quite a bit about myself and my company to her. This gave me an opportunity to talk with her about some of the different people at the company and what they did. I took notes on names and job descriptions. By the time she transferred me to the person she thought I should talk to, I had names of two others who worked at the company and what they did. It wasn't much but it was a beginning.

A big part of research is simply keeping track of the people you come across. It doesn't do you any good to make a contact in a company or find out about a company, if you don't remember it later. A good practice is to develop a filing system for keeping track of people by the company they work for. There are a lot of great software programs out there for keeping track of contacts, but I have found that what works best for me is to add them to my contacts list in my email program. Some of the new web-based email programs even allow you to access your contacts anywhere you have internet access.

Networking

One of the best ways to get to know people at a company is to network. *Networking* is the process of talking to people you already know to get to know the people they know. The idea behind networking is to have someone you know introduce you to someone you want to know. There is an implied endorsement in this scenario that helps to increase the chance you will be successful in your efforts to make friends with the new acquaintance. Introductions are very powerful in the business world. In some social circles and in some cultures it is the only way you can do business. In countries like Japan there is very little cold calling because it simply is ignored. If you want to do business with a company, you have to be introduced to that company. The more influential the person is who introduces you, the more seriously you will be taken by the company. It is just the way business is done in that area of the world.

While countries outside of Asia may be more likely to listen to a cold call and in some cases even be willing to meet with you, you are still many times more likely to get that first meeting if you are introduced to the company by someone who is respected by the company. So if networking is so powerful, how do you do it effectively?

One of the best ways to network is to just talk with your friends and acquaintances. These are people who already know and respect you. Mention that you are looking for business opportunities with certain companies and ask them if they know anyone who works there. By being straightforward in your approach, you can actually get them thinking about their own contacts and who might be best to introduce you to. For the most part people like to help one another. If they like you, they will likely want to help you.

Networking is a two way street, though. If all you do is take, you will find fewer and fewer people willing to help you. If, on the other hand, you also are willing to help others and introduce them to people that you know, they will often return the favor.

It has been said that we are only three people away from anyone we want to meet. While I know of no way to prove that, I do believe there is a solid principle there. The idea is that within one's circle of acquaintances, there is likely to be one or more people who know someone that knows the person you want to meet, no matter who that person is.

In recent years there has been a rise in the popularity of social networking websites. These websites, such as MySpace, Facebook, and LinkedIn, provide a way for people to interact and network with each other in an online setting. While they will never be as good as face-to-face meetings, they are great tools and can give great results. One of my favorite networking sites for business is LinkedIn. The reason I like LinkedIn is because I can find an individual that I want to get to know and then trace how I might be able to be introduced to that person by people I already know. I can ask someone within my own network to introduce me to someone who is outside my network but in theirs. Sometimes the people I want to speak with are one introduction away and sometimes they are two. I haven't found many that are more than two, but occasionally there are a few.

Building Recognition

Earlier we talked about good will and how it can be used to influence people at a company. Building recognition is much the same as building good will. The idea is to find ways to get your name or your company's name in front of the decision makers of the companies you want to work with. While the focus of creating good will is a little different in that you are just trying to increase the good feeling a company or its employees have toward you and your company, *building recognition* is the process of being admitted to the business circles of the people who run that target company.

One of the major differences between a small company and a large company is the role the owner plays in the company. Small companies generally are associated very strongly to their owners, in fact many of them are identified with the owners. You often hear something like "That is so-and-so's company." On the other hand, very few large companies have one specific person that they identify with. It is only on rare occasions that will you find that the company is identified by its owner.

Because smaller companies are so closely associated with their owners, name recognition of the owner is almost as good as name recognition of the company, and in some cases it is even better. Business owners who build their own companies often are admired by other business executives. Building a successful business of any size is not an easy endeavor; it takes a lot of work and perseverance. While all business executives may not dream of building their own business someday, there are many who do. If you are an integral reason for the success of your small business, you likely already have some level of respect from other business executives. The more well-known your business is the greater that respect can be.

Good public relations for a small business can go a long way to help that business gain notoriety and recognition in the business community. Along with growing revenue and profits, you should also consider developing a good public relations program that gives your business a chance to be seen and heard. Becoming a respected member of the community and supporting community events is one way to build that recognition. Other ways are to join and participate in local business organizations or clubs. Not only do these groups provide you networking opportunities, they also give you chances to get yourself and your business in front of other business executives.

Being in the Right Place at the Right Time

In the end, a lot of business opportunities come about by just being in the right place at the right time. Some companies may have the people who anticipate problems and look for solutions well before a problem actually arises, but it is more common for a solution to be sought only after the problem occurs. Because people tend to deal with current problems rather than future problems, there is usually an urgency to solve what they are facing. That urgency creates an opportunity for the small business owner who can be there to solve the problem when it arises.

Being in the right place at the right time may sound like happenstance, but it doesn't have to be. What it really amounts to is being the first company a business manager thinks of when faced with a problem that your company can solve. You don't actually have to be standing right next to the person when the problem occurs; you just have to be the first person that comes to mind. In our local area there is a small chain of stores that deal with window replacement. One of their slogans is "When you hear the crash, think of Jones Paint and Glass." They are trying to promote the idea that if there is a broken window, they are the ones who can fix it. Over the years the association of their company with the repair of a broken window has helped to sustain their business.

When faced with a problem, a manager in a large company has two critical objectives: solve the problem and solve the problem quickly. The longer a problem continues to be a problem, the more likely it will reflect poorly on the business manager whose job it is to fix it. Managers are under a lot of pressure to maintain deadlines and ensure the smooth operation of the company. If there is a viable solution to their problems right at their fingertips, more times than not they will jump at that solution rather than doing an extensive search to find a less expensive solution.

To be in the right place at the right time requires that you are known by the company in relation to the problem and that you are aware of what problems larger companies may face.

We have already covered the importance of being known by managers in a large company. The point here is to be known for a reason—in other words, your company is associated with solving a particular type of problem. This means a more targeted approach to name recognition. You want name recognition that includes association with particular problems or solutions. Just like the glass store, you want your company to be the first to come to mind when a particular problem surfaces at a company. For example, if your company deals with internet promotions in specific geographical locations, you want businesses to think of your company first when they need to promote their products in your location.

One thing that is often overlooked by small businesses is the necessity of keeping pace with the needs of large businesses. If you can anticipate a need, you have a chance to be there when that need becomes a problem for the company. For example, suppose the government passes a new law requiring the registration of a part used in commercial jets. Anticipating that a lot of complex paperwork will be involved in the registration process, you contact the branch of government and arrange to train your company to deal with the registration. When you complete that training, you are in a position to contact aerospace companies and offer your services.

Anticipating the future needs of large companies will likely require you to become familiar with the current needs of those companies. It is amazing how much you can learn from managers in casual settings if you take the time to listen. Sometimes even in meetings you can learn about what the company may need simply by asking. Industry news is another good place to find these types of opportunities.

The First Meeting

Okay, you have passed the gatekeeper and you have a meeting scheduled with the company you want to partner with. First meetings with a company are important. They can make or break your chances to form a partnership because they set the tone for all subsequent meetings and negotiations to come. Before you walk into that first meeting there are a number of things that you should consider.

- Know your objectives
- Do your homework
- Out-numbered and on foreign soil
- See things from the point of the view of your partner
- Work with middle management and/or gatekeeper
- Ask questions
- Be sure you can walk away
- Is it a pitch or a partnership?
- Learn to listen
- Be prepared
- Be flexible
- Always address the key business measures
- Tell a story
- Show that you have vision

Know Your Objectives

In every meeting you attend, you need to know your objectives—objectives for that meeting in particular as well as your overall objectives. In a first meeting, objectives need to be tempered with an understanding that you are just beginning and there is a lot of ground you need to cover before you reach the finish line. You may hope that the whole deal can be negotiated in one sitting, but that is highly unlikely. Most first meetings with a large company are primarily fact-finding meetings, and there are no real expectations for making a deal at that meeting from their side. Large companies are slow moving, so you should expect several meetings before you finish a deal. If you push too hard for a deal in the first meeting, you will likely appear desperate.

Your real objectives for the first meeting should be to create interest in your company and what it has to offer and to set the stage for future negotiations. Your presentation should be well rehearsed and crisp. It should contain only those things that will inspire interest in a partnership and not anything that is deal specific. That will come later after you have captured their interest.

If they want to know what kind of deal you are looking for, you have a good sign that they are interested. You should have a good idea of what kind of deal you want before you enter the meeting and be able to articulate that deal clearly, but it is always better to have them ask for it than to just make it part of your presentation. Sometimes it can work to your advantage to have them present a deal first.

I recently spoke with a friend about a deal he made with a much larger company. Before he and his partner entered the room, they agreed on what they wanted, and they also agreed that they would not make the first move; they wanted the company to come to them with their idea of what a fair deal was first. During the meeting the company asked several times what they wanted. Each time they deflected the question back to the company. Finally the company made an offer. The company's offer was twice what they had agreed upon before they entered the meeting. It makes later negotiations go much smoother when you start at twice the price you were hoping for!

Do Your Homework

It will be a red flag to the company you approach if you really don't know anything about them. They won't expect you to know their inner secrets, but they will want to know that you have at least a basic understanding of their operations. If you can show that you have taken the time to understand the company and you already know who the top executives are, you may even impress them.

The real reason you should do your homework before you enter that first meeting is so that you are prepared for and understand how they will approach the negotiation process. This takes some investigation and it might even mean contacting other companies that have met with them in the past. If they are hard negotiators, knowing that before you meet will help you to be better prepared. If they are slow movers and seldom tip their hand early, that is also good to know. If they present a happy, positive face to everyone but only do deals with one or two companies a year, you can manage your expectations.

Out-Numbered and on Foreign Soil

When you first walk into the meeting it can be a little intimidating. For one thing, most first meetings will be at the company you want to work with, which means that you will be walking away from your comfort zone and into theirs. In all likelihood you will also be outnumbered at the meeting. In my own experience, large companies tend to have a number of people attend the first meeting. This isn't so much a tactic to intimidate as it is to make sure that anyone who might be interested in the partnership is present. It is much easier for interested people to be at the meeting together than it is to try to tell them about the meeting later. I have often found myself outnumbered four or five to one in most first meetings.

There is a famous history lesson about a group of 10,000 Greek mercenaries between the third and fourth centuries BC. The story unfolds as Cyrus the Younger challenges his brother Artaxerxes II for the throne of the Persian Empire. Unfortunately Cyrus was killed in the decisive final battle, stranding the 10,000 Greeks deep in enemy territory near the ancient site of Babylon. Their march home through hostile territory and overcoming incredible odds is one of the most notable military stories in history. The Phalanx infantry fighting methods they employed changed the face of battle for centuries to come and were the backbone of Alexander the Great's armies and later the Roman legions.

The decisive difference between the Greeks and the armies they had to contend with was that the Greeks were superiorly organized. They had an objective and a system that worked as a single unit to reach that objective. They understood their opponent and understood what they had to do to win their way home. Your first meeting with your potential partner isn't and shouldn't be a battle, but the principles of good organization and understanding your potential partner will give you an important edge.

Even though you may be out-numbered and on their turf, you still can come out of the meeting feeling good if you are well organized and know your partner.

See Things from the Point of the View of Your Partner

One of the reasons that we have spent so much time in this book talking about the structure and culture of large business is to help you to see things from their point of view. To be a good partner you have to understand your partner. The more you can look at the partnership from the large company's point of view, the better you will be able to address their concerns.

When I first started in business, I used to get upset about some of the things I had to deal with when I worked with bigger companies. One of those issues was that it often seemed that milestone payments would be held up on what to me seemed like small technicalities. Later, when the shoe was on the other foot and I was the one making the deal with the smaller company, I saw that I only had a limited amount of money in my budget. It didn't matter if the project took longer to accomplish, I only had a certain amount of money and that was that. If the project wasn't finished completely, I had to account for that money. I realized then why milestones had to be complete. If they weren't complete, I ran the risk of having the entire project shut down.

By taking the time to see things from the partner's point of view, you are also reinforcing that you believe their point of view is important. It is encouraging to them when they see you have that understanding.

Probably the most important aspect of seeing things from their point of view is that it will enable you to speak to those issues that are most important to them. It helps you to know what to say and how to say it.

Work with Middle Management and/or Gatekeeper

The first meeting will probably include a number of middle managers as well as the gatekeeper you worked with to set up the meeting. There may be an upper level manager, but don't count on it. The upper level managers will more than likely appear later in your second or third meeting with the company.

From the larger company's point of view, this first meeting is to determine whether your company has something to offer them. Unless they called the meeting to address a specific problem they need to solve in a hurry, their attitude will likely be that they are doing you a favor by seeing you. Be careful that their attitude doesn't unduly influence your perception of the meeting. It is normal for a large company meeting with a smaller company to take the superior role, however, most of the time I have found it to only be a minor irritation.

Pay close attention to the people you are introduced to in the meeting: who they are and what they do. One of the first things you should do is trade business cards. Lay the cards out in front of you and keep track of names and job titles. Remember that the one doing most of the talking may not be the one who has the power to make decisions.

Ask Questions

If any partnership is to occur, a lot of information must be shared between the two companies. In this first meeting you should ask a lot of questions about their company. Talk to each person in the room and ask them who they are and why they are at the meeting. Take notes of important answers, especially from those people who have a specific reason for being there.

This first meeting is not merely an opportunity to get to know each other; it is also an opportunity to learn *why* people are at the meeting. Each person at the meeting will have a reason to be there, but not all of them will be there because they need your company or want your services. Some of the people at the meeting may have their own agenda and some may be there because they think the company *doesn't* need you.

I once attended a meeting with a large company where I met with three middle managers. I was invited by the two higher level managers but a third manager wanted to be at the meeting, too. As the meeting unfolded, I recognized that this third manager saw me as a threat to his own agenda of where he wanted the company to go. He liked things as they were and was only at the meeting to defend what he perceived as his own turf. His feelings were very strong and I wasn't able to convince him that I wasn't a threat, however, had I not asked several questions during the course of the meeting, I may never have learned about his attitude.

Over the years I have learned that most meetings are pleasant but not all of them are productive. Sometimes there are roadblocks that need to be overcome. Sometimes there are preconceived notions that have to be dispelled. In any meeting situation it is best to set the expectation for honest and straightforward conversation. Ask questions and listen to the answers. Ask if they have partnered with other companies like yours before. Ask if those partnerships were successful. Ask if what you offer is already being done inside the company. Ask how they evaluate potential partners. These questions and others can help you learn their motivations, which in turn can guide you in how you should present your company in later discussions. It will also help you to see if there are problems that you need to overcome.

Be Sure You Can Walk Away

Even though it is just your first meeting, a bad deal will not do your company any good. Sometimes in the heat of a negotiation or presentation, the desire to make something work can get carried away and you might be tempted to make a commitment you can't keep or promise more than you can deliver. You may find yourself rationalizing and accepting a company's request just to get them to agree to a deal. This temptation can be overpowering, especially when the deal may bring your company a lot of new business. Be careful. Never take a deal that you will regret later. Sometimes in these first meetings the company is probing to see what you will do when asked.

Before going into the meeting, give yourself guidelines about what kind of deal is acceptable and what kind is not. For example, write a list of items that are important and keep them handy so that you can review them during the meeting if you need to. Your list might look like this:

1. Profit margin has to be no less than 20%.
2. Company name must appear on product packaging.
3. Retain ownership of company patents.
4. Must have 20 day lead time on all orders.
5. Retain ownership of company.

This list is just an example but it covers several key areas that you should consider, such as profitability, publicity, intellectual property, working relationship, and company ownership. While your list will likely look very different, you should consider those particular areas.

Make sure every item on the list is of high importance. If you can live with some adjustment to the list, like 15% profit as opposed to 20% profit, then give yourself a little leeway. Don't turn down a deal because it is just a little off, but do turn down a deal that will be a problem. Going over the list will help you to make the right decision.

Only desperate people need to take bad deals. The company you are negotiating with knows that and they may just be testing to see how much they can get. You need to be prepared to walk away from a bad deal. If they really want you they will be willing to compromise.

Never be pressured into making a quick decision. If a deal is good today, it will still be good tomorrow.

Is It a Pitch or a Partnership?

If you prepare a presentation for the first meeting with a slick PowerPoint presentation and flashy graphics, it may come off more like a sales job rather than a partnership proposal. You should be prepared, but making a presentation that is a production may do more harm than good.

Pitches Seldom Really Work with Senior Management

Senior level managers have lived through a multitude of presentations. They tend to want to talk with real people rather than sit through a flashy PowerPoint presentation. Some of them view presentations as a waste of their time. I recall one meeting where the senior manager didn't want us to give him a presentation at all. Instead he just asked us a few questions, explained what he wanted, and then left. The junior level managers were expected to work out the details. He had already looked us up and made a decision about the deal he wanted before the meeting even started.

In most cases slick presentations come off too much like a sales pitch. No one likes being talked at rather than talked to, and this is especially true of a senior level manager. Keep your presentation simple with bullet talking points. When a question arises, be flexible enough to answer the question even though it might interrupt the flow of your presentation. The presentation is a communication tool not a major motion picture.

Learn to Listen

The most important thing you will do in your first meeting is listen. Even if they ask you to present your idea and want you to jump right in, leave plenty of space for listening to what they have to say. As much as you want to get your great idea for a partnership across to your audience, you need to hold back and let them talk.

You learn a lot more about a person by listening to them than you do talking to them, and the same principle holds true for companies. When you listen you invite them to share information that might be valuable and useful in the future. I remember a conversation with a colleague of mine who made an interesting observation about meetings with potential partners. He made the comment that in almost all of the meetings he attended, the deal he eventually made with the companies almost never centered around his proposal. The proposal only seemed to open the doors to the company. Once he was inside and meeting with the people who made decisions, they usually had completely different projects that they wanted to do. This comment was interesting to me because the individual was successful and had completed more than a dozen partnership deals, some with very large companies. Much of his success was attributable to the fact that he *listened* to the needs of his partners and understood that they were looking for a solution to a specific problem that they had. By showing a willingness to deal with their problem he was successfully able to walk away with a partnership.

Be Prepared

The Boy Scout motto is as applicable to business as it is to scouting. Being prepared for the meeting will greatly enhance your chances for a successful outcome. Being prepared doesn't mean creating a flashy presentation; it means to come prepared to talk about a relationship between the two companies. You need to have knowledge of your potential partner's company and of the subject of the discussions. In particular, this means bringing help with you to the meeting if you feel you won't have the technical answers they need. In my business there is a technical side and a creative side as well as the business side. Because my background is in business and creative, I don't always feel comfortable fielding technical questions. The last thing I want to do is appear ignorant in front of my potential partner, so I bring a technical person with me when I meet with potential partners. Having someone there to talk about the technology helps me to focus on the areas I know best while not appearing unknowledgeable in the meeting.

You should be the expert on your company and the proposed partnership, but you should also come prepared in other ways as well. Being prepared means that you've done your homework, you have a basic knowledge of the partner company, and you've taken the time to read up on any recent industry news. It means that you know what your company wants, and it also means that you have more than one way to partner with them.

Be Flexible

Flexibility is important when developing a partnership. I haven't found many situations where one type of deal will work for all partnerships. One thing that I like to do before attending a meeting is to go over the possible ways that I might be able to partner with the company. I run through several scenarios in my mind to help me to not be so rigid in the meeting.

I once attended a meeting in which we were discussing a specific point. We had implemented the same solution for others but this company wanted something different. We presented several ideas to them but none of them seemed to fulfill their requirements. Eventually, after a great deal of discussion, we jointly came up with an idea. The new idea was untested but it was much less costly to implement. By letting our partner know that we were flexible, we were able to come up with a better solution.

Always Address the Key Business Measures

In Chapter 4 we talked about the key business measures that are so important to large companies:

- Return on Invested Capital (ROIC) and/or Return on Investment (ROI)
- Revenue and volume growth
- Profit growth
- Market share
- Customer service
- Working capital
- Total delivered costs
- Speed to market
- Effectiveness of new products
- Quality

When you have that first meeting, make a point to address as many of these key business measures as you can in your presentation. When you do, you will be speaking their language in terms they will understand.

Tell a Story

You may think, "Why tell a story in a business meeting? What story should I tell?" These are good questions, so let me explain. Every year in the area where we live they hold a storytelling festival. Not long ago my wife and I attended the festival and I was reminded again of the power of storytelling. Storytelling is more than just talking about a series of related events. The art of storytelling is the ability to bring something to life in the minds of those who are listening. A master of the craft can take a mundane event and relate it in such a way that it captures the imagination of the listeners and transports them to the location of the story.

A good story has a strong beginning where the storyteller captures the listener's attention. Good stories have powerful plots that pull the listener along, building excitement for the finish. A good story has a message that resonates with the listener. And finally, a good story has a strong finish that completes the experience.

The primary story you want to relate to your listeners in your first meeting is the story of your business and why you think a partnership is a good idea. When you talk about your business see if you can put it together in story form. Don't make it too long, but do make it have feeling.

People love to hear stories. I work on the board of directors for an entrepreneur club in our area. We invite a speaker to come every month and address the club. Usually the speaker is a successful business person who has built a great business from scratch. When we ask members what they want to hear most from these individuals the response is always business war stories. They want to hear a story. We've tried to bring in good, informative presentations and while the content is appreciated they just don't score as high in the members' minds as a story does.

Stories are memorable. Facts, figures, and formulas are not memorable. When you present ideas as stories or use stories to illustrate your points, you create something that the listeners will remember. You give them a way to remember you, your company, and your proposal. A good story can stay with someone for a long time.

When telling a story you need to make sure the story directly relates to the point you want to make. Many of the executives you will talk with have a steady diet of PowerPoint presentations and stories from the best in their industry. After awhile they often become jaded and not interested in listening to rambling stories that only loosely relate to the topic.

Recently while trying to explain how a new game we were working on could be played by very young players, I told the story of how I had brought the game home and had my granddaughter play it. She was only 4 years old at the time. I explained how with only a little help from adults she was able to play the game. I told how she played the game for more than half an hour without stopping (a very long time for anyone who knows 4-year-olds) and how she started to cry when her mother told her she had to go home. I finished the story by telling how I had to promise to give her a copy of the game when it was finished in order for her to be willing to stop playing. The story was very effective in getting my point across.

Be careful to not get so carried away with your storytelling that you forget that listening is more important than talking. Use stories to help make your talking memorable and interesting, but don't overuse them.

It is also important that you practice your stories in front of an audience. You don't have to have them memorized, but if you find that you are nervous when speaking to a group, you might forget an important part of your story. Running through it a few times will not only help you in your delivery, but asking for feedback may help you refine what you present and emphasize important aspects of the story.

Show That You Have Vision

We often think of someone who can see the potential in something as having vision. A visionary is someone who can see possibilities. When expressed well, one's vision can be communicated to others who may not see the possibilities or potential in a business idea. People with vision are respected in the business community because it is their vision that maps the course of companies. People with strong vision usually rise to the top management positions in the company. To be a good leader you have to have a vision of the potential in those you lead and in the concepts you embrace.

If you want to catch the attention of top managers and those who will be top managers in the future, you can do so by expressing a clear and powerful vision of how you think your partnership with them will work to benefit both companies. More importantly, if you can't visualize clearly to yourself how the partnership will benefit the companies, how can you expect to articulate it to others in that first meeting?

Take some time and map out a vision for your company. In a way it is like dreaming, but dreams with direction and a path to get to them. If you are like me you have imagined what your company could be. Close your eyes and see if you can picture in your mind what your company will look like in five years. What kind of building will it be in? How many employees will it have? What kind of name recognition will it have? You don't have to be realistic in this exercise; reality can come later once you have your dream. For now just take a moment to dream and see if you can see a vision of what your company might be. The blue sky dream is helpful because it gives you the beginning of a goal. Yes, it might be totally impossible, but the impossible has been known to happen.

As with any dream, at some point you have to wake up and do the work to make that dream a reality. Now that you have your dream, break it down into its different aspects. For example, the building you imagined: What would have to happen for you to get into that building the way you imagine it? What level of revenues and profits would you need to sustain it? What types of changes have to be made to reach that level of business?

The simple activity of dreaming can put a lot of things into motion. One of those things is likely to be looking for a good partner that can help you achieve your dream. By seeing the possibilities you start to build a vision for the future. By working out the roadmaps to that vision you bring reality to the vision. After you have those two components, you are in a better position to communicate your vision to others.

Common Mistakes

In addition to the things that you should do in your first meeting, there are several things you should avoid:

- Talking to the wrong person
- Being too emotionally invested to see their point of view
- Failing to remove the owner for the first couple of meetings
- Being unprepared
- Being too scripted: not listening
- Having poor presentation skills
- Letting them see you sweat

Talking to the Wrong Person

Talking to the wrong person means that you spend a lot of time talking to someone who has no real power and can't help you much. This comes from two things: You don't understand the person's position in the company, or the person misrepresents what he really can do. Sometimes it is both. It is pretty frustrating to work with someone who you think can open the door to a good partnership only to find out later that that person has no real power to do it. It is also frustrating for the person you are talking to when you ask him to do something he can't.

The only real way to avoid talking to the wrong person is to do your homework on the power structure of the company. See if you can determine the titles of the individuals involved and understand how they all fit together.

Sometimes you may find yourself in a meeting not knowing who the boss is and what everyone's roles are even though you attempted to do your homework before the meeting. In that case, you might just need to ask. I have often just asked outright, pointing to another person in the room, "So are you his boss?" This almost always brings a response and opens the door to a short discussion on who everyone is and what they do. It doesn't always work, but it does most of the time.

Being Too Emotionally Invested to See Their Point of View

Sometimes we become too invested in our company and how things are done. To us, we may see no reason to change things because we think our current system is perfect. We can also become too invested in our company to the point that we see any changes as a threat to the company or the company culture. These feelings can sometimes cause us to become defensive. Know that anytime you become defensive in a meeting, especially a first meeting, you have probably lost the partnership.

The problem with defensive behavior is that it shows inflexibility and weakness. Defensive behavior can completely change the dynamic of a meeting. I've seen this happen in several meetings over the years. One of the people at the meeting feels that he or his ideas are being attacked or diminished. Instead of listening openly to the discussion, he hunkers down and starts defending his point of view. He is no longer listening and seems to only be able to focus on one thing. You don't ever want a meeting to stall because of you or someone on your staff. Even though you might be presenting your life's work, you must be able to distance yourself from it emotionally so that you don't feel the need to defend it. This will help keep the meeting positive and productive.

Failing to Remove the Owner for the First Couple of Meetings

This may sound harsh, particularly if you are the owner. It isn't that the owner isn't important, it has more to do with the fact that most of these first few meetings are brainstorming sessions where lots of ideas are considered. Sometimes, these ideas are so far away from what you want as a partnership that those who have high investments in the company start shooting them down, which takes us back to the emotional investment problem again. There is likely no one more emotionally invested in a company than the owner of that company. It may be a mistake to have the owner there if you know for sure that there will be problems. If you are the owner, don't make the mistake of thinking you have to be at the meeting.

A good way to avoid the negative ramifications of too much emotional involvement in the first few meetings is to have trusted managers attend these meetings and then report back to the owner. This way they can have an open, frank conversation with the owner after the meeting in a less stressful situation. It also creates an opportunity for the owner and those who attended the meeting to evaluate different ideas away from the presence of others outside of the company.

A side benefit of keeping the owner out of the first few meetings is that later, when higher level managers start to attend the meetings, the owner can attend and put him or herself on an equal footing with the high-level managers. It is kind of like when the President of the United State wants to visit a foreign country: an advance team is always sent to get the detailed negotiation resolved so that the leader can just sign the agreements when the President arrives.

Being Unprepared

We have already talked about how important it is for you to do your homework before you come to the meeting. While doing your homework can be a great benefit, I also need to point out that lack of homework can be a big negative.

I remember taking a trip to look for partners where I scheduled several meetings with a number of companies in Southern California. I didn't do a lot of homework and just scheduled meetings with any company that would accept me. One meeting, in particular, didn't go well. They were pleasant enough, but they were just a U.S. front for a foreign company that only wanted to import their products and was not interested in making project partnerships with U.S. companies. Their main question to me was, "Why are you here?" I didn't have a good answer. Why was I there? Because I didn't do my homework.

Being Too Scripted: Not Listening

We talked before about the dangers of having a too flashy presentation and turning your audience off because they feel like it is just a sales job. Another danger is to have your presentation too scripted. What I mean by that is that you become so engrossed in presenting to the exclusion of everything else. This is dangerous because when you are in presentation mode, it is more difficult for you to listen.

Over the years I have listened to a lot of public speakers. Some were very good and some were not so good. A good public speaker has a way of grabbing the audience's attention and holding that attention while he or she delivers their speech. These public speakers don't read from a script. Many of them don't even have their speeches memorized. What they do have is a list of points that they want to make. They use the list but talk in their own voice to the audience. Because they are talking to the audience and not reading a rehearsed script, they are able to gauge the interest of the audience and react to it.

Like a good public speaker, you need to be able to gauge the interest of your audience and change your presentation as needed while you are talking. Unlike the public speaker, you have the opportunity in the meeting to ask questions and get direct feedback. In other words, you also have the chance to listen to others in the meeting. Don't squander your chances for a good partnership by reading from a script or turning everyone off because you are talking about something that doesn't interest them.

Having Poor Presentation Skills

One reason that people write out a script for a meeting is because they don't feel comfortable speaking in public, even if that public is only a dozen people around a conference table. For the most part, just relaxing, being yourself, and being prepared will go a long way to giving a good presentation, however, it may not always be enough.

If you are serious about being a partner with a large company and you feel that you need to be the one who makes the deal, you may need to get some help to upgrade your presentation skills. Taking public speaking classes from a local university is always a good idea. Getting a public speaking coach can also help. At a bare minimum you should rehearse the presentation before a live audience, even if it is just others from your company or your family. The more times you go through it with others watching the more comfortable you will feel. It also helps if you have them ask a lot of questions that they feel might come up in the meeting. This will help you to respond well to those questions.

Letting Them See You Sweat

One of the biggest mistakes you or anyone on your team can make is being too nervous to present yourselves and your company well. When you are nervous, others often start to feel nervous as well. It doesn't matter why you get nervous. Getting nervous will always be a turn off in a meeting. As humans, we have to learn to detect emotion. I once wrote a book on capturing emotion in animation. The point of the book was to help animators learn to draw emotion in their characters. In animation emotions are exaggerated but what is interesting to note from my studies of emotion is how adept we are at reading emotion in others. For example, take a look at these simple drawings from the book. Can you tell what emotions the characters are feeling?

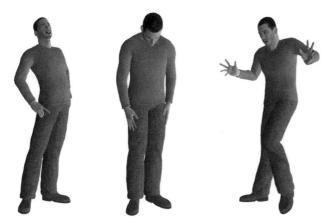

Figure 6.1 *What emotions do you read from each character? Image created by Les Pardew.*

If you can read an emotion from a simple drawing, what do you think you can do in real life? We learn how to read emotion in others at a very early age. A child learns early how to tell whether Mommy is happy or sad. Some people are so adept at reading emotion that they can sense the emotional state of anyone they are near.

In that all important first meeting, you need to project an air of confidence and trust. Emotions like anger, fear, resentment, apprehension, and the like have no place in the meeting if you want to reach your goal of making a good partnership.

I've found over the years that nervousness comes from inexperience for most people. Other people have social anxiety, and the only way they can overcome it is to seek professional help. If you are one of those people, I suggest you talk with your doctor to find help. If, on the other hand, you are like most of us, you just need a little time and practice to get your meeting feet under you. Some other suggestions are to take a public speaking class at your local university and to volunteer to speak at functions in your community. Anything that gives you a chance to speak in front of groups will help you to feel more comfortable doing it in a meeting.

Don't make the meeting so important that you stack so much pressure on yourself that you can't help but be nervous. With experience comes the knowledge that there are very few meetings in a person's lifetime that are so critical that everything is riding on it. Some may seem like it at the time, but they seldom really are that critical. Taking a longer term view of things will help you to put your meeting in perspective. The worst thing that is likely to happen is that you will fail and not get the partnership at this time. There will be other partnership opportunities and other companies you can approach.

Recently I had a meeting where I was to demonstrate some technology to one of the biggest companies in our industry. Making a partnership with this company has always been on the top of my to-do list. I really wanted to make a good impression. However, as I got the technology up and running I noticed a major bug. I had given the presentation a number of times and the bug had never happened before, but wouldn't you know it right when I needed things to work the most, there it was. I could feel myself starting to sweat, so I turned to the leader of the group I was presenting to and said, "You know the only time something breaks is right when you are showing it to someone important." He smiled back at me and said, "I know exactly what you mean." From then on, the presentation went much better.

The Second Meeting

It is always exciting when you get that second meeting. The second meeting means that the company is interested and they either want more information or they want to introduce you to other people in the company. While it is a good sign, don't think the deal is done yet or that it will be done after this meeting. You are likely to have many more meetings before the deal is finished. Here are a couple pointers for that second meeting.

Get an Agenda

While the first meeting is almost always a get to know each other meeting, there are any number of reasons for holding a second meeting. The company may want you to talk to another division. They may want to explore your ideas more deeply. They may just want to let you get to know them better by showing you some of their people and facilities. This second meeting could be about anything. Don't go into it blind; ask for an agenda.

An agenda will help you prepare for the meeting, and it will also help you to understand their intent in holding a second meeting. Usually the company will tell you why they want a second meeting but having an agenda will put those reasons down on paper so you can study them beforehand and develop strategies for each item. Without an agenda you are walking into the meeting blind.

Asking for an agenda also gives you a chance to place items that you want to discuss on the agenda. Because the agenda is sent out in advance, you can request that certain topics be placed on the agenda before the meeting.

Understand the Audience

From the second meeting on you will see two things happen with regard to who will be attending the meetings. Your meetings will be either working meetings or approval meetings. Sometimes these two meetings will be combined, but most of the time they will not.

A *working meeting* is a meeting filled mostly with lower level managers who are working with you to iron out details on how a partnership might work. Their interests will be in how things will work between the two companies. These meetings may be in the field or on location either at their company or at yours.

An *approval meeting* will have high-level managers who are there to basically meet about making the partnership real. They may be interested in details but it is more likely they will want a broader view of the arrangement.

As in the first meeting, it is vital that you know who you are talking to and how they fit in the overall power scheme of the company. If you are unsure, ask. From experience I have learned to ask people in the room what their role in the company is at the beginning of a meeting. I have seen and heard of many business meetings where the presenter gets so caught up answering questions from someone who doesn't have any real say in the partnership—and ignoring those in the room who have the real power—that the rest of the people in the meeting become bored and lose interest.

By asking people what their role in the company is at the beginning of a meeting you not only give yourself insight into who the real powerbrokers are, but you also remind those in the meeting where they fit. If they know that you know their role, they tend to not try to dominate the meeting. However, that doesn't always work. In some cases you have to shut the person down by saying something like, "can we stay on topic here" or " I thought this meeting was about _____." Looking at the person in charge from the other companies helps get the point across.

You should also know who you are talking to so that you can deal with the issues that are important to them. For example, if your meeting is with the CTO (Chief Technical Officer), you probably don't need to go into a lot of financial detail. On the other hand, the CFO (Chief Financial Officer) will want a lot of financial detail. If you are unsure what will be covered in a meeting, work out an agenda with your contacts at the company beforehand. Again, having an agenda will help you plan for the meeting.

It's Just a Second Date, Not a Marriage Proposal

If you are married, you probably didn't propose to your spouse on your second date. In all likelihood you dated for awhile before the proposal came. You may have known by that second date that you wanted to propose but you probably wanted to check a few things out first before you felt ready to take such a big step. Partnerships in business are similar. While everyone might feel like the partnership sounds like a good idea, you are probably going to have many meetings before you close the deal.

Like dating, there is a courting process that must happen to arrange a good partnership. During that courting process both you and your potential partner need to learn everything you can about each other. This will take time. Don't expect it to happen overnight. The art is to keep things moving without seeming to push too hard. A good question to ask if things seem to be taking too long is, "What is the next step?" Try to find out what they need to do and what they expect you to do. That way you can measure progress.

Be a Little Hard to Get

Things seem to work out best in business negotiations if you know how much the other party wants the deal to happen. If you are always the one pushing the deal, you will never really find out how much they want you. If, on the other hand, you let them do some of the pushing, you may get a better idea.

Being a little hard to get can really work in your favor because it will cause your potential partner to have to do a little work to gain your company as a partner. This can have the effect of sweetening the deal as well as move things up the ladder more quickly. It may seem counter intuitive to hold people off a little, but in the long run it actually can speed things up.

A business consultant told me the story of a doctor who was having trouble finding new patients. He was a good plastic surgeon but he just couldn't seem to get enough people interested in his services to keep the doors open. After seeing how his business was being handled, the consultant suggested that instead of scheduling a patient on the first available appointment opening to require at least a month wait for an appointment. The doctor didn't like the idea because he had openings available right away. The consultant told him that wasn't the point; his problem had to do with public perception. A sign of a good plastic surgeon was that they were booked months in advance. By holding people off a few weeks he would actually create a better public perception.

The doctor gave it a try and made a rule that all appointments had to be scheduled at least a month out. Eventually perception became reality and he became so busy that he couldn't get someone in sooner even if he wanted to. By being a little hard to get he increased his value in the eyes of his customers.

In most situations you are better off talking to two or three other companies in your search for a partner. Not only does this give you a sense of stability, it also gives you options. You don't have to take any one deal. You have the luxury of being able to pick the best deal. It is all part of strengthening your position.

Negotiation

If you are going to progress to creating a partnership, at some point you will finally have to negotiate the nuts and bolts of the deal. Usually negotiations are a process and take a lot of work and refinement before they are implemented. During that process there can be a lot of distractions and questions. It always seems to take longer than it should and seldom comes off without some compromises on each side. However, if you stay focused and patient you can get through the process with a minimum of casualties.

Preparing for the Negotiation Event

In some cases you will be invited to a meeting to go over the deal points and finalize an agreement; you will talk about those areas that the two companies need to come together on in order to make things work. Usually a lot of the negotiations have already taken place by the time this meeting is called, but that isn't always true. Some companies will want to sit down early on and explore everything. Whatever the meeting is, you should go prepared.

Take the Right People

The last thing you want to happen during a negotiation is to appear unprepared. Calling back to the office to consult with a technical person or your CFO can make you seem unprepared and take away any edge you might otherwise have had. Don't go into a negotiation by yourself. It is as important to get buy-in from your own people as it is from your potential partner. Take those people to the meeting who can give you support and help to answer any questions that might come up.

Who Makes the Decision?

It is important to know who makes the decision and who makes the recommendations in any negotiation. When I say decision, in this case I mean the final decision to accept the partnership deal. Is that person you or is it your company's board of directors? Don't fall into the trap of assuming that because you are the owner you can have the final say excluding everyone else in the company. If it is your company and you have complete control, then yes, you can make the decision, but don't expect everyone to be happy about it if they don't have any say in it.

By the time you sit down to negotiate a deal, make sure you have talked through all of the major deal points with your top management and investors. By doing so you can address their concerns and define the parameters within which a decision can be made. This will give you some guidelines. As long as you stay within the guidelines you can feel confident that you can make the final decision and have everyone on board.

Who Does Most of the Talking?

There should be one person designated to do most of the talking in a meeting. This will help present a more unified front to those you are negotiating with. It doesn't mean that others in your group can't talk; it just means that most of the talking should be from one person. Usually the best person for talking in the meeting is the one who understands your company's objectives the best. In all likelihood that should be the company president or chief executive officer, but it can be someone else if everyone feels that person can do a better job.

If issues come up in negotiations that need private conversations, request to talk with each other privately for a short time. It is better to argue among yourselves off line than to do it in the middle of a boardroom.

Tell Your Partners to Stay Away or Stay Silent

The partners I am referring to here are not your potential partner but other stakeholders in your company. If you invite them to the meeting, you need to clear the air first about who will speak for the company and who will not. The last thing you want is a verbal disagreement between stakeholders in your company during an important negotiation.

Know What Is Really Important to You

We talked earlier about knowing what issues are important. Let's go into that in a little more depth to help you keep those issues in the forefront of your mind during negotiations.

Exit Strategy

Understanding a partnership from beginning to end is important in any negotiation. At some point your partnership will end, and you want it to end in the best way possible. During the negotiation process, define how the partnership can be terminated so that both parties understand how it will work. You want to be sure you have a way out of the deal if things go bad as well as if they go well. If they go bad, you want to be able to stop things before there is damage to both companies. If things go well, you want to be rewarded for a successful partnership.

Long Term versus Short Term

Every partnership needs to look at both the short term impact of the partnership and the long term implications. Before you go to the negotiation table, make sure you understand that what is acceptable now may not be acceptable in the future.

As of the writing of this book there is a significant lawsuit between Vidal Sassoon and Proctor and Gamble. What started out as a great partnership has turn into an ugly court battle. At the heart of the battle is Vidal's claim that P&G has devalued his brand greatly, thereby affecting the brand's worth and his royalty potential. P&G claim, on the other hand, that the brand is old and tired and their attempts to revive it have failed.

Vidal Sassoon's rise to fame was hard fought. The man, who at one time was synonymous with high fashion hairstyles, started out life as an orphan in London. He swept floors in a beauty solon as his first job. Through hard work, charisma, and boldness Vidal developed a chain of beauty salons and a set of products that brought high fashion hairstyles to the forefront of public awareness. Celebrities from many fields, such as fashion models, actors, political figures, and singing stars, all looked to him for the latest in hair fashion.

The partnership between Vidal Sassoon and Proctor and Gamble was supposed to be a match made in heaven. In the beginning it was just that, but as time wore on the Vidal brand lost much of its luster. While the courts will have to sort out who is really at fault, the fact is that neither party is happy right now. They seem to be stuck with each other and neither one likes it.

The point is that companies change and so does the market. What will happen to your partnership if things change? You need to think through how changes might affect the partnership and plan for ways to deal with those changes.

Are You Desperate? Could You Really Walk Away from This Deal?

This is a very important question to ask yourself before you go into a negotiation. In a perfect world, you would be able to choose from a variety of partnerships and not be compelled to accept any one. However, we don't live in a perfect world.

I remember a point in one of my companies that we were looking at the real possibility of having to shut the company down. We had gone several months without any revenue and had reached the end of our credit line. It was during this time that I had to negotiate one of our biggest deals, and I was desperate. My company was desperate. I was ready to take a deal no matter how bad it was just to keep the doors open. It was a difficult place to be and I hope you never have to go there.

What I learned through that experience is that even though I was desperate, I didn't have to act desperate. I also learned that what might seem like a desperate time may not truly be one. Often our problem as business owners is that we don't look down the road far enough. I decided to not worry about the state of my company. I only looked at the merits of the deal and evaluated whether it made sense for us to take on the partnership. As it turned out, the deal we made was a good one and it was the beginning of our company's recovery.

Later our partners talked to us about the negotiations and mentioned that they had no indication that we were desperate at all. I never did tell them that we were. As a company owner you have to separate yourself from the pressures of your company to make sure you can make the right decision and not the desperate one.

What Are the Real Dealbreakers for You?

As mentioned earlier in this chapter, you need to make a list of those things that have the potential to kill the partnership. Doing so will help you to keep your priorities straight in the negotiation process. Some of these dealbreakers may not be completely cut and dry. In some cases you may be able to live with one issue if you get something else in return.

One partnership we negotiated with a company asked us to forfeit any royalties for a product that normally had huge royalty potential. Their rationale was that they had to pay so much money to the licensor for a celebrity endorsement that they just couldn't justify a royalty in the product. We were ready to walk away from the deal when one of the managers approached us with a generous bonus plan that essentially gave us the same revenue potential as the royalties but just under a different system. We decided to go ahead with the partnership and it worked out fine.

In any list of dealbreakers it is important to know what truly is a dealbreaker and what may only appear to be a dealbreaker. Often what seems important at first glance is only a want-to-have versus a must-have. Put some real thought into your list before you make it final.

Control: Can You Relinquish It?

No matter what your partnership might be, whenever you make a partnership you relinquish some control. That is just the nature of a partnership. You have to expect that. However, in some cases, such as the purchase of your company or a majority investment, you may find yourself giving up control of your company completely. Are you ready for that?

For many small business owners, giving up control of their company is like selling part of their body. They were the ones who fought and worked to build the business. They are the ones who know the customers and know what the company needs. To give up control will put the business in the hands of someone who hasn't had to go through all the growing pains. However, the fact is that sometimes giving control of the company to a good business partner with greater resources and market reach might be the best thing for your company.

I can't say what is best for every business; that is a decision that you will need to make yourself. What I can say is that if you make that decision, you must be prepared to deal with the consequences. You will no longer be calling the shots. You will have to learn to let others lead. If you can't do that, then maybe as part of the partnership you should leave the company and enjoy the rewards of your hard work.

Are You Willing to Let Them Take Your Product and Not Take You?

Sometimes your partner might only be interested in your company's product and not in a partnership with your company. In these instances the larger company sees a way to use their market reach to take a good product to the masses. They want control over the product and only want to have a financial obligation to you and your company. If that is the case, then the partnership between the two companies is very different than if the two companies were working together. It doesn't mean that the partnership is a bad deal; on the contrary, it might be the best deal you can make. It just means that you need to understand how it will impact your company.

In some cases, a royalty deal can bring in a lot more revenue than trying to build the market for your product on your own. The upside to a royalty deal is that they do all the work and all you have to do is collect a check. The downside is that they now have full control of the product and the brand. As in the case of Vidal Sassoon mentioned earlier, they may not have the same passion for the brand as you do.

Can You Work within a Corporate Structure?

Some partnerships tie the two companies so closely together that they become one company. In those cases, you may be required to become a manager within the large company. Is that something you can live with?

A wise attorney who had dealt with a number of company purchases by large corporations made the comment that he hadn't seen many successful assimilations of company founders into large corporate structures. His recommendation to our group of entrepreneurs was to negotiate a great golden parachute because we were likely to be fired. His point is that company founders don't usually make good corporate citizens.

Know What Is Really Important to Them

In addition to knowing what is important to you, a good understanding of what is important to your potential partner can help you immeasurably in your negotiations. Often learning what is important to them comes only through a lot of experience working with large companies, but there are a few things that you can pick up that might help if you know the right questions to ask.

How Well Does This Partnership Meet Their Needs?

To understand how well your company meets their needs, you first have to understand what those needs are. Ask them to list the reasons they are looking at your company. If they are willing to do that, you can then compare what they are looking for with what you really have to offer. That can help you to see what their expectations are.

Short Term versus Long Term Needs

You need to understand if your company is a short term solution or a long term partner. If all you want is a short partnership and they are looking for a long term arrangement, there will be problems. If, on the other hand, you want a long term partnership and they are just looking for a short term solution to a problem, you will not like the results.

Some companies will be upfront with you about their intentions. The best companies will want you to know what their plans are so that you can plan accordingly. Other companies will not be so forthcoming. For these more secretive companies, you will just have to look at their track record and see what they have done in the past.

Do They Need You, Your Product, or Both to Make This Work?

If they need both you and your product to make the partnership work, they will likely talk about getting both at the onset. However, I have seen situations where the large company wanted only the product at first, but after learning about the company they decided to buy the whole company. Sometimes the reverse happens and they decide that only the product is needed.

If the large company is looking at your partnership as an investment, they will be significantly more interested in buying part of your company than they will in investing in a single product.

If all they want is to leverage their marketing, they may only want your product. Knowing their motives before you start your negotiations can help you manage your expectations.

What Are Their Hot Button Issues?

Hot button issues are the top line critical aspects of the partnership for the large company. Finding out what the hot button issues are will usually take some investigation, as they may not be willing to share that information openly. What I have found in my own negotiations with other companies is that honesty begets honesty. If you talk about what is important to you, they will often return the favor. Listen carefully to what they say.

You can also test the waters a little to see how they react. I remember a partnership in which we were going to create a product for a larger company. In the course of our negotiations I pushed things around a little by suggesting that we move the completion date a little. They wouldn't budge. I then tried to push the project costs and found the same unmoving wall. Finally, I started talking about features and found that they were flexible in that area. My investigations helped me to understand that they had a fixed budget and a commitment on the completion date but they were not tied to specific features. This information helped me a great deal in crafting a partnership proposal for them.

Have You Clearly Addressed Each of the Key Business Measures?

Again we need to refer back to the key business measures as stated earlier in this chapter and in Chapter 4. When you talk about these key business measures, you are speaking a language that your potential partner is going to understand. On a scale of one to 10, how do you rate your ability to deliver on each of these and how important is that element in closing this deal? Try rating them yourself, and if you are really brave and have a good rapport with your potential partner, try rating them together.

Win/Win

Always approach the negotiation from their point of view while at the same time ensuring your needs are understood and addressed. Both companies need to do well in the partnership or the partnership will not last.

Sometimes it is a good practice to open with a statement about wanting to reach a win/win arrangement in the partnership. This puts the other negotiating party on notice that you are not trying to just see what you can get but that you will listen to their point of view and do your best to adjust things to work for them. It also establishes that you expect them to do the same. See if you can get them to agree at least verbally to wanting a win/win solution. That way if things start to get sticky later you can always refer back to the opening statement.

Be Open-Minded

There are a lot of ways to do things. Never assume that there is only one good way to form your partnership.

One time I was working on a three-way partnership. One company was a software publisher interested in publishing our software; we will call it Product A. Another was a programming company that had some technology that we needed for Product A and the ability to adapt that technology to fit the software product. The third company was mine. The problem we ran into was how to get the money it would take to get the development work done. Everyone liked the idea but we were stuck without a way to fund the development.

After a little creative thought we came up with a solution. The publisher had some technology that I could use in another project, Product B, that we were working on at the time. To get the technology, I was going to have to license it from them anyway. I also needed a programming group to adapt the licensed technology so that my client could use it.

We decided to do a three-way investment. I paid the programming group to create what I needed and paid the publisher the licensing fee. Instead of keeping the licensing fee, the publisher gave the programming group the fee as an investment. The programming group then had enough money to create both products. Because I brought the money, I got my Product B for my client and also got a portion of the profits on Product A. The publisher was able to get Product A without any out-of-pocket expense. The programming group got the money they needed to work on both Product A and Product B.

As you can see, with a little creative thought and open-minded negotiations, we were able to come up with a solution that enabled us to move forward.

Be Realistic: How Much Do They Really Need You and Your Product

The fundamental question here is "Is your partnership critical to them or is it just a nice-to-have partnership?" Of course, the best position for you is to be the critical solution they are looking for, but that doesn't always happen. If the partnership is critical, they will be willing to make more concessions to ensure that the partnership is good for you. If the partnership is less critical, then they will not be so willing to make concessions and may even want you to make concessions.

Be realistic. Don't think that you are more important than you actually are. Yes, you want to make a good deal for your company, but if you have an inflated idea of your value to your potential partner, you are unlikely to come away with any partnership. A key component to a win/win arrangement is for both parties to understand how important they are to the other party.

The other side of the coin is that if your potential partner feels like they are more important to you than they really are, they, too, can have an inflated sense of their value. The best situation is for both parties to recognize that they don't have to have the partnership but maybe with a little bit of work on both sides the partnership can become something that both parties feel like they have to have.

Learn to Work through the Problems

I have seen too many instances in which negotiations seem to hit a wall and one or the other parties gives up. The truth is that nothing good is ever free and nothing worthwhile ever happens without a lot of work. You may be tempted to pack it up and move on. Sometimes that will be your only option. However, I've found that setting a good foundation for the negotiations and showing a willingness to listen and understand my partner generally helps us get through the problem areas.

The key to solving problems is to understand them. Sometimes you just need to figure out what the real problem is. Ask questions if you don't understand. I remember negotiating a deal with a foreign company. They had all kinds of problems with their country's taxes. One of the issues was that they had to pay a tax for every payment they sent us. This meant that the fewer payments they made the less overall tax they had to pay. We were used to getting paid on a regular basis for the projects that we undertook. We worried that if we let them get too far behind, it could leave us in a bad position financially and unable to pay our own bills.

With a little creative work we came up with a payment solution that worked to save them on the tax payments and ensured that we didn't get behind on our own payments. We didn't know about the tax issue when we proposed our payment schedule. Because they were a foreign company and didn't speak our language, it took a little work to find out what the real problem was and then find a solution.

Language That Works and Does Not Work

You may have a thick skin and not get offended by the way someone talks about you or your company, but you can't expect those you are negotiating with to feel the same way. For any negotiation you need to be careful what you say and how you say it. I've seen a few times where the whole negotiation process ground to a halt because of something someone said.

Profanity

While a cuss word here or there might seem funny or even lighten the mood in your company meetings, it has no place in a serious business negotiation. You should avoid any word or expression that could be considered profane, obscene, or vulgar.

Argumentative

Have you ever been in a meeting where it seemed like one of the people there wanted to pick a fight? It can get very uncomfortable very fast. Argumentative language is language that causes arguments. In most cases it is a defensive stance that someone takes because he feels threatened, but on occasion it can also be offensive, in that the person is taking the first shot in a battle.

Negotiations are not battles and should never be viewed as such. If you feel threatened, it is better to stop the negotiation and come back to it later. Getting angry in a meeting will only cause regrettable words to be spoken.

Don't Use Negative Labels

Don't ever use negative labels about people, ideas, or businesses. One message that comes across loud and clear is that if you are willing to talk negatively about someone or something, you are likely going to talk negatively about them to others. As the old adage goes, "If you can't say something nice, don't say anything at all."

Positive Words

One challenge of any negotiation is to keep things positive. Positive is an attitude but it is also the words you choose. Give compliments to jobs well done. Let the people in the meeting know that you appreciate their attendance. Be quick to say you like something if you do. And above all be courteous. Don't try to talk over someone else.

When to Walk Away and When to Run

Not every negotiation will work out and not every partnership will work either. Sometimes you just need to walk away from a deal even if you have invested a lot of time and money in it. If the deal doesn't meet your original objectives or it misses on most of them, there is a high likelihood that you are going to have a problem that won't get resolved by forcing a partnership.

Some red flags to be aware of in your negotiations are problems with individuals, deal structure, expectations, and illegal activity.

Sometimes the best companies have bad employees. There are cases where a bad employee can totally ruin a good partnership. Take a hard look at who you will be working with and make sure they are compatible with your company.

Some deal structures are just not good for your company. For example, your company might need to have a consistent cash flow. It is common for a large company to want to make fewer payments and take longer to pay them. If you don't have the cash to wait for your money, you may need to look for a better partner.

Expectations in business are always high; however, your partner may be expecting more than your company can give. If this is the case, you are headed for a disappointed partner and a bad partnership. Make sure you can deliver what your partner expects.

One situation that you should get out of as fast as possible is if you suspect any illegal activity. Usually this is not a problem when dealing with mega corporations but there are some large companies that try to skirt the law from time to time. It might be just one manager but it can be a big problem for you if you make a partnership with them. If you think something isn't right, run as fast as you can.

The Final Deal

If everything works out in your negotiations, you are on your way to making that partnership. It is likely that there will be a partnership agreement along with a number of other documents and forms that will need to be completed before the partnership can happen. Let's take a look at a few of them.

Working with Purchasing: Another Negotiation?

If the partnership includes payment for services or products, you will likely have to work with purchasing and have to deal with purchase orders. This means that you need to register with them and provide all the important information that they need to send you money.

In a large company they will have a separate department called purchasing that deals with payments. Purchasing controls all outgoing funds from the company. They usually have a whole list of procedures and rules that you will have to follow. Sometimes what they need might be at odds with what you negotiated. If you have anything that is unique about your partnership, you will have to work with your partners and purchasing to iron them out.

Terms and Conditions

Hire a good attorney. Don't skimp on having someone who understands a partnership agreement. You are making a significant business agreement that might span years. You don't want to miss the meaning of some term in the contract or have some unexpected condition present itself. Take the time to read the agreement yourself and flag anything that might be questionable. Then have your attorney do the same.

You should always take the time to understand the entire contract. Of course, you want to get started as soon as possible. You have worked hard to get to this point and it is natural to want to get the partnership moving, just don't do it at the expense of not understanding the contract. It can come back to haunt you later.

Working with Their Attorney

When you are working on the partnership agreement, you will work with their attorney and not the people with whom you negotiated the deal. In most cases it will be wise for you to have your attorney talk with their attorney. Have your attorney report back to you about any issues that arise and make sure he or she understands what you want and what was negotiated.

Their attorney may not have been in any of the negotiation meetings. It will be important that you take good notes in those meetings so that if there are any promises made, they are included in the agreement. Their attorney will only be able to go on what was written down and any instructions given by those who attended the meetings.

Remember that their attorney is tasked with protecting their company and will approach the agreement from that standpoint. While the people you negotiated with were more interested in the business arrangements, the attorney is focused on the legal ramifications. There will likely be quite a bit of back and forth before you can get all of the legal issues ironed out.

Never Change the Deal After the Negotiation Is Over

After you negotiate the deal and it is signed you won't be able to change it. At least you won't be able to change it right away. If you were smart, you may have set up an annual review of the partnership where you can make changes, but for now will have to live with what is in the contract. You will look very unprofessional if you come back after the contract is signed and ask for a change. Even if you do ask, it is very unlikely that you will get the change. It just takes too much work for the large company to go through a change process.

For your own sake and the sake of your company, take as much time as you need to ensure that the contract is good and that you haven't missed anything. I can't stress this enough.

Get Moving!

You've done it. You've made your partnership and now it is time to make the partnership work. In the next chapter we will cover what to do now that you have your partnership.

Chapter 7

Keeping the Romance Alive

So you signed the contract and now you have the partnership you wanted. It's time to celebrate, sit back, and watch the revenue roll in, right? Well maybe you can celebrate a little, but in reality your work is just beginning. Making the partnership deal, as challenging as that was, is only the beginning. Now the real work begins.

If you can't make the partnership work in practice, your great deal is really worth nothing. A great partnership is not just a contractual arrangement; it is a living, breathing, working relationship that has to be cared for if it is to succeed. To really make your partnership work you have to do just that—go to work.

Rather than just working and hoping that you build a good partnership, though, there are several things that you should know to help you build your partnership in a way that solidifies your reputation with your partner and places you in the best position for any new partnership opportunities.

In this chapter we want to cover important aspects of how you can build a great partnership. We first discuss how your management contacts will change and how that will affect your ongoing operations. We will talk about why there will be a change in management during the work phase of the partnership and how you can best deal with it.

Another important topic that needs to be addressed is the importance of integrity in a partnership relationship. We will talk about why you need to train your personnel to treat the partnership the same way they treat your one company's internal management.

Communication is a critical aspect of running a good partnership with another company. We will cover why communication is important and give you some suggestions on how you can create a good communication system.

With every partnership, there will be expectations. Some of the expectations will be promises that you or your employees make to your partner. Other expectations may simply be implied. We will address why it is important to keep promises and how you can deal with implied promises.

Keeping the partnership a win/win relationship will improve your chances of having a good long-term partnership. We will endeavor to help you maintain a strong win/win relationship with your partner so you can build that great relationship that brings better and better opportunities for you and your company.

Sometimes things change. No partnership will last forever, but that doesn't mean that you can't change the partnership to adapt to changes in markets, company direction, and other factors that will come up. We will try to help you set up a system that gives you a way to periodically review and adjust the partnership.

Finally there will come a time when the partnership has run its course and you need to move on to other partnerships. We will talk about how you can disengage gracefully, leaving the door open for other future opportunities.

For any small company going into a partnership deal with a large company there will be a few surprises, some pleasant and some not so pleasant. If you know what you are getting into, though, you will be much better equipped to take advantage of the good surprises and at least minimize the damage of the bad ones.

New Managers to Work With

In most large companies there is a distinct difference between those who negotiate the partnership and those who manage the partnership. One of the responsibilities of senior management in most large corporations is to negotiate and finalize partnerships with other companies. However, they generally turn over the day-to-day running of the partnership to middle management. For the most part this is a good thing, or at least it is a good thing if you are prepared to deal with it.

In a large corporation, high-level management have to split their time between a number of pressing issues and projects. Their role in the company is to focus on the bigger picture and not get involved in the details; they hire middle managers to take care of the details. This frees senior management to direct the operations of the company with greater perspective. It isn't that they are not interested in the partnership they just made with your company, it is just that they can't devote the time necessary to make the partnership work on a day-to-day level. In fact, I would be skeptical of a situation where a high-level manager is running the daily functioning of the partnership; most of the time it doesn't work.

In one partnership I was a part of, we had a senior level manager that wanted to run the partnership from the larger company side. He was very enthusiastic about the project and wanted to make it his own. At first we loved the idea that a senior level person would take such a personal interest. As time passed, though, we found it more and more difficult to keep the project moving forward because there were many small issues that came up every day that needed his attention. Our manager was a very dynamic and busy person. Even though he had great intentions, important decisions often took more time than necessary, which caused delays to progress. As time went on it became obvious to everyone that we needed to have someone assigned to the project for daily care and only take the big issues to our senior manager. Once the change was made the project ran more smoothly.

Having a mid-level manager working on your project can really speed things up because they will have more time to devote to your project and will be more accessible when problems or questions arise. You can still go back to your original company contacts should major issues develop, but you can save those relationships for the big issues and do the day-to-day work with others who are better equipped for the job.

Middle Managers

To understand why it is best to work with a mid-level manager, it is important to understand what the role of a middle manger is in a large corporation. In a large company there are many managers, sometimes hundreds or even thousands in really big companies. The management structure of the company is hierarchal, with line managers reporting to mid-level managers who then report to senior managers. In some companies there are many levels of management, with each level reporting upward to a higher level and managing downward lower levels of managers.

The idea behind a corporate management structure is to give everyone in the management hierarchy a manageable workload while maintaining a high level of productivity. This means that the lower a person is on the management scale, the more specific and detailed their job becomes. The higher the manager, the more general and supervisory their job becomes. Day-to-day operations are handled by lower level managers who oversee very specific aspects of the work. They then report their progress to mid-level managers who are responsible for several work projects and have a number of other low-level managers reporting to them. Higher level managers have several mid-level managers reporting to them and they in turn report to yet higher level managers until it reaches the top level company executives. While every company has its own management system, they generally tend to work in the same way.

It is easy for someone outside of the large company to get confused about who manages who and who reports to whom, and this can be particularly frustrating for the small business owner, who may feel like they are being passed from one person to the next in the company with no one making a decision on important matters. This frustration can be eliminated to a large extent if the small business owner will take the time to learn about the management structure of the partner company. For example, learn about your counterpart at the large company. What is his or her official title and what responsibilities go with that title? What authority do they have for expenditures and authorizing work from their end? Who do they report to and what is that person's role in the company? What types of decisions can they make on their own and what ones do they need approval for from a higher manager?

Larger companies have multiple people working at multiple tasks. For example, you may have a person who you contact for partnership-related work issues and a completely different person who you contact for payment or marketing issues. It is very likely that depending on the issue involved, the manager you work with directly may not know many answers to any question outside his or her direct responsibility.

Most managers have limited freedom to act within specific guidelines. The better you understand the limitations placed on a manager, the easier it will be for you to work with them. You won't end up asking them to do something they can't do, which would only cause frustration for both of you.

The best way to find out about a company's management system is to ask a lot of questions. Doing so upfront will save you a lot of trouble down the line. Ask the high-level manager to fill you in specifically on what your new contact can and can't do. Throw out a few scenarios and ask how they should be handled and by whom. Try to understand what issues can be handled by the new manager and what ones you need to direct to the higher level contacts you have.

Try to get the names and contact information for all the major areas that you may have to deal with during the partnership. You can use the following list as a guide:

- Legal issues (if there is ever a legal question you need answered)
- Marketing issues (if your product will be marketed by them)
- Payment issues (if you will be receiving payments from them)
- Procurement issues (if you will be receiving products or assets from them)
- Transportation issues (if you are required to travel)
- Product approval (if you are delivering products to them)
- Project oversight (if you will be working directly with them)

These are just a few of the more important issues that you may need to deal with during a partnership. Depending on the type of partnership, you may have more. A good thing to ask is, "Who else should I know at your company that I don't know now?"

Management Problems

I was in a partnership with a large company where the manager responsible for our project was causing us some real problems. His division had been taken over by a new boss; the new guy brought in a bunch of his own people and there was a distinct rift between the new managers and those already in place. Many of the old managers were let go, causing great apprehension on the part of our manager. He was so concerned about making a mistake that he delayed approval of our work for long periods of time to try to keep his expenses down and appear to the new boss to be tough. This, of course, delayed payment to our company and started to make the whole partnership unprofitable.

At first we tried to work with the manager, but the more we pressed the more stubborn he became. As time went by the project became more and more difficult to execute. Eventually we had to make a choice: either approach his new supervisor or drop the partnership all together. We decided that we still wanted to have the large company as our partner, so, as painful as it was, we arranged a meeting with the new supervisor to discuss the manager.

I don't recommend going over your manager's head; you should do so only when you reach a point where problems just can't be resolved. Going over someone's head will usually cause resentment and sour a relationship. In our case, we told ourselves that either they gave us a new person to manage the project or we couldn't continue the partnership. After we made that decision, we moved forward with talking to his boss.

When dealing with a problem with a manager it is best to come prepared with all your evidence and to not attack the manager but rather attack the problem. Focusing on issues rather than personalities leaves room for negotiation. No matter how frustrated you might be with an individual, you will only make enemies if you attack someone at your partner company.

In dealing with the situation outlined above, we pointed out that it would be in the interest of both companies if approvals were not denied without specific reasons. We requested a more defined system for approvals that included a line item task completion list that we both could check. We did everything we could to take the ambiguity out of the process. We did request a fresh start with a different manager from their end, but we stated that we would also change the management on our end as well. They agreed and we were able to successfully continue the project.

Not all management problems are as drastic as the example above, but there are almost always some growing pains as the two companies start to work together. If problems do occur with a specific manager, it is best to try to work things out directly with that manager. It is also best to work it out as quickly as possible. What may seem like a small problem in the beginning can turn into a major disaster if it isn't addressed right away. Methods of working together quickly turn into routines that are hard to change down the line.

The best way to work through problems, whether with a manager or otherwise, is to establish an attitude of "Let's all work together to get this right" at the beginning of the project. Schedule regular reviews with your partner in which both parties can speak freely about how the process is going and the relationship in general. As you examine each aspect of the partnership, rate how each partner is doing with an eye to how they can be improved. This will help set the stage for dealing with problems. It will also show a willingness to listen to how things work in your partner company. You can learn a lot about your partner in these meetings. You will also learn a lot about the people you work with.

Finally, don't expect perfection. There are a lot more moving parts in a large company than there are in your small organization. Things that only take minutes may take days with your behemoth partner. It is better to anticipate longer lead times with them than to get upset with what appears to be simple matter. For the most part, middle managers work hard to do the best job they can within the constraints of their company. If you can make them your friend and are understanding of their role, you will likely be pleasantly surprised by what they can do. They can become your chief advocate with the company. Remember, too, that successful middle managers are often promoted within the company. A good relationship with them can be very important to the future of your relationship with your partner company.

The Importance of Integrity

There may not be anything more important in a relationship between partner companies than integrity. Integrity is the foundation upon which you build a lasting relationship. Without it neither party can trust the other, and without trust your partnership will not succeed.

Trust is not something that you will just automatically have with your partner. Trust is something your partner will not just automatically have with you. Trust is something that is developed over the course of your partnership. It is gained by the trustworthy actions of both companies as they work together through their day-to-day dealings with each other. It can be damaged by any action that is perceived to be less than honest by either party.

Perception is important. Regardless of the intent or even the reality of the situation, if an action is perceived to be anything less than absolutely honest, it builds distrust and suspicion between partners. This is true for any partnership, not just business partnerships. This may seem a little unfair but fairness has nothing to do with it. It's just the reality of the situation. That is why you have to be doubly certain that you look at everything your company does from the perspective of your partner.

While you can't control the integrity or trustworthiness of your partner, you can control your own dealings and ensure that your company is always scrupulously honest in all your affairs both toward your partner and to everyone else. Word gets around. If your company is perceived to be honest by everyone who deals with it, your partner will likely hear of it. A reputation for honest dealings is invaluable in the business world. It is one of the only ways a company can establish trust before working with a company directly.

Taking Advantage of a Situation

In business there is a lot of pressure to make a profit, and this pressure can result in trying to find any way possible to increase margins to improve profitability. However, in a partnership the idea is to work together so that both companies are more profitable, not for one company to profit off the other (or at their expense). While a certain amount of profit is expected for any company to prosper, problems will result when one company takes advantage of a situation to drain money from the partnership. When I say drain, what I mean is that one company hides the true cost of something from the other company in order to jack up the price and increase the margin. The problem with this type of practice is two-fold. It artificially increases your prices beyond competitive levels, thereby opening the door for other companies to take your business. It also gives you a reason to hide your true costs of doing business from your partner.

If you charge your partner for services or products and you build in a profit margin that is higher than your competitors might be willing to sell that same service or product, you set yourself up for a failed partnership. No matter how hard you try, you can't keep your partner from learning the true costs involved. They are eventually going to find out either from their own investigation or from overtures from your competitors. When that happens, you will often find that your partner will either want you to match the price, if you are lucky, or they will leave the partnership for a better deal with someone else.

The idea of a partnership is for both companies to make profits together. Usually sustaining a good partnership over a number of years will result in greater profits for both companies than the few items you might be able to profit from in the short term. It is better to work out a true and realistic rate for any service or product your company supplies. This will build trust in your company and engender a greater degree of loyalty in your partner.

In Chapter 3 we talked about how to protect your company's assets while in a partnership with another company. One of the ways to protect your company is to maintain trade secrets. Secrets are powerful because they deny information to all except those who know the secret. While it might be important to maintain trade secrets and keep that information secure, too many secrets kept from a partner can and often do have a negative effect on the relationship between the two companies.

Secrets about the true costs of goods or services you might supply to the partnership can lead to distrust from your partner, particularly in the situation when they find out about the true costs. Think about it. If you paid $50 for a cleaning product from one of your suppliers and that supplier indicated that they were giving you the best price possible, and then you find you can actually buy the product from someone else for $25, wouldn't that change your perception of the supplier? Believe me, they will find out. No matter how tightly you might try to contain that information, it will get out. All it takes is one disgruntled former or current employee, a spurned wife, or an aggressive competitor to spill the beans. You might as well be open and let your partner know what the true costs are and what you need for a profit margin on products and services you supply.

In the best partnership arrangements both companies are working toward a common goal, which is to create and market a great product or service that will be a category leader for years to come. For the product to be successful over the long run it must be competitive in the marketplace against all other products and services of the same nature. Therefore, artificially increasing the development or production costs of the product does not serve the best interests of the partnership and will likely shorten the life cycle of the product or service.

In most partnership situations it is better for both parties to deal with real costs and agree upon reasonable margins in an open and clear way. That way there is a better chance for both parties to make profits when the product or service goes to market and have greater price flexibility when other companies try to compete in the same market.

Every situation is different and you as the company owner must make the right decisions when it comes to pricing your company's work, but in almost all cases it is better to not jump at a quick profit jeopardizing a much larger future profit.

Taking advantage of your partner may not be just in money or profit margins. Sometimes you can take advantage of information or the good will of your partner. For example, you may in the course of your interaction with your partner learn information that could be useful to your partner's competitors. Even if this information is not under a confidentiality agreement, you should not divulge that information to anyone. Competitors may ask for the information and they may even offer some attractive incentives for information on your partner, but divulging it will only cause you to lose the confidence of your current partner and the respect of the competitors. Those competitors know that if you will divulge information to them, you will also do the same if you were their partner.

Sometimes a partner will offer to let you or your employees take advantage of facilities or other perks that they have like company recreational properties or spa memberships. While that is a great gesture, it has a cost to their bottom line. Overuse by you and your employees can cause resentment from your partner's employees, especially if you are taking time away from them. It is best in these instances to define how much use they are really offering and then make sure you never go over those limits.

In business, as in life, your best choice will always be to be honest. Good business practices like honesty, standing by your word and your product, using the best materials and building the best product, offering the best service, and keeping your promises will give you the best chance for success in your partnerships. A good reputation will bring you more long-term profits than any short-term advantage you might be able to take.

Hiding

When dealing with a partner, your employees may be tempted to color the truth in an effort to make your company look better or because they are dealing with a problem that they don't want your partner to know about. In both cases, while they may be trying to look out for the best interests of your organization by looking at your partner as an outside entity, in truth their efforts will cause you more problems than just the issue they are trying to cover up. Just as it is important for your employees to be upfront about any problems or situations with internal management, it is also important that they not hide anything from your new partner.

The problem with hiding is that it has the potential to damage trust between companies. It makes your counterpart at the partner company ask, "Why wasn't I told about this issue?" and may cause them to wonder what else they may not know. Little problems tend to grow into big problems. If everyone is aware of a problem while it is still small, it will have a better chance of being resolved early, and in the case in which it isn't, your company may not be held solely responsible for the costs of the larger problem. For example, consider the situation in which there is a shipping problem with parts for a product your company is building. Because the parts are late, it causes your team to be late delivering the product, which in turn means there isn't enough product for a special promotion scheduled with a major retailer. Because the retailer had a penalty clause in their contract, your partner has to pay a significant penalty for not having the product available on time.

If you had communicated the problem right away when you learned the parts would be delayed, you could have worked together with your partner to solve the problem. Your team might have assumed that being a few days late wouldn't cause that big of a problem, but they didn't know about the penalty clause because they didn't share the information with your partner right away. If your company had been forthcoming about the initial delay, you and your partner may have been able to resolve the problem and have enough time to make adjustments to production or negotiate a change in the promotion time.

Not only does hiding the problem negatively affect your partnership, it also denies you the opportunity to learn. The types of problems you experience are not unique to your company. Product delays and underestimating how long it takes to get a job done are common issues in any company. Larger companies deal with these problems so often that they develop systems and ways of handling them. If you are upfront about issues as soon as they arise, you might be surprised to learn that your partner can help in ways you never thought of. For example, one of the partners we worked with had some problems getting a response from a company. I just happened to know one of the leaders of that company and placed one phone call to them. They responded within minutes of my call. Never underestimate the power of having a big partner on your side.

While your partner may not need to know about every little issue, as a rule over-communication is better than not enough communication. A good way to think of this is that you are both trying to manage a process. Your company has some of the responsibility and information and your partner has some of the responsibility and information. Together your companies hold all of the responsibility and have all the information. Neither company can work alone; you need both companies to get the job done. Therefore, learning to communicate issues accurately and honestly with each other isn't just a nice thing to do. It is a critical thing to do.

Communication

Communication is vital to any relationship and any management structure. If you have employees at your company, you probably spend a significant amount of time communicating with and receiving communication from them every day. Good communication within a company can help the company to be more efficient and help everyone who works there to be more productive. It can resolve problems and increase the likelihood that your company will be able to take advantage of opportunities as they arise. In the same way that good communication is important inside your company, it is also important with your partner companies.

You need to think of your partner as an extension of your own company. They are partnering with you for a specific goal that both companies share. To make the partnership work with the same degree of effectiveness as your own company, you have to communicate on the same level with them that you do within your company. Obviously the communication will be limited to only those aspects of your operation that have a direct effect on the partnership, but within that narrow band communication should flow freely and openly.

A good practice in defining communication with your partners is to determine during contract negotiations or when you first meet the managers you will be working with what level of communication they want from your group. In my experience, a weekly written update is usually about right, but every company will be different. Either you or another person that is assigned to manage the partnership from your company's side should prepare the regular updates. These updates should be organized in such a way that they are easy to read and understand. An effective way to do this is to arrange them into bullet points that deal with specific aspects of the work being performed. The following is an example of such a report for a software project.

PROGRESS REPORT FOR XYZ APPLICATION

05/15/2009

Overview

The team has made good progress toward an Alpha build that we expect to deliver by the end of the month. They fixed the crash bug that had delayed last week's progress build and they also integrated a new routine for parsing user input so that almost all the features are working now. We feel that we are about three weeks behind our original schedule and will need to move the remaining milestones out that far. We also anticipate needing more testing in the coming weeks.

- We were still having what appeared to be random crashes of the program, but John was able to isolate the problem thanks to your testing team's help and fix the bug. As we suspected, it was caused by a memory leak.
- The new user input parser was integrated into the application and now the other features are working with that code. We ran it through several internal tests and everything seems to be working well. Please have the testing group check it out and let us know if they come across any problems.
- We are continuing to work on the other new features and should have them in place in the next two weeks.
- As a whole the project is roughly three weeks off its original schedule. We had planned for some unforeseen issues, but hadn't anticipated that there would be so much trouble implementing the search features.
- The delays in development will require that we push back the remaining milestones at least three weeks. We feel confident that we can meet that schedule barring any other unforeseen issues. We don't feel we will be able to make up any time at this point as the team is already fully tasked.
- We anticipate as we go into the next several weeks that there will be a bigger need for testing and need you to schedule additional time with the testing team. We are planning to send two builds: one on Wednesday and one on Friday of next week. Please have them ready for those builds.

The preceding example is a brief weekly progress report. It is obviously for a small software application and isn't extremely long. You will notice that there is an overview that states in one paragraph all the important issues. Then each issue is given more detail in a bullet list. This type of report is easy to read and also easy to write. It also keeps your partner current on the progress of the project and aware of the schedule. Notice that it gives the partner company a heads up on when progress builds will be delivered so that they can schedule testing time. Your own progress reports may be longer or shorter depending on the size and scope of the work involved. To be safe, you—as the primary decision maker for your company—should always review any communication with your partner to ensure that it is accurate and includes all important information, as well as any additional information they may have requested.

There are many reasons to create and deliver regular written progress reports, not the least of which is that it leaves a paper trail that can protect your company in the event of a dispute. The partner company will not be able to say they were unaware of problems or issues regarding your company's work. Those issues will be in the progress reports and if they were reported promptly, you will be able to show when each issue occurred and when the partner was notified.

Formal and Informal Communication

In any partnership there should be both formal and informal communications. Formal communications are usually written. They can take the form of progress reports as mentioned, but they might also be accompanied by presentations or other face-to-face communications. Informal communications are usually verbal, but they can also be a text message, instant message, or an email, and they may or may not deal directly with the progress of the partnership. There are so many more ways to communicate today than there were only a few years ago that defining formal as written and informal as spoken doesn't work all the time.

When dealing with formal communications, it is very important that the communication is reviewed by you prior to delivery to your partner. The reason is that formal communications become part of the official record in case there is ever a need to review the partnership. Official formal communications between companies carry more weight than other documents. This is because it is assumed that an official formal communication was thought out carefully before it was sent.

It is highly likely that all written communication be they letters, emails, or memos will be saved by your partner even if it is just a "hello, how are things going" kind of communication. Even if you don't think of the communication as formal, they might.

Formal communications can play an important role if there is ever the need for legal action. It is a good practice to maintain an archive of all written communications between your company and your partner company. You never know when you might need those records. They are certainly keeping track of yours.

As an example, one of the companies that we had a partnership with was being sued by another company they were partnering with. The lawsuit was directed toward the work that we had done for them. They were claiming that there was an infringement on some of their intellectual property and they had the courts place an injunction on the product that we had developed. Fortunately we had kept records of all communications between our group and our partner company. With the help of those records we were able to show that we had actually developed the product independently, which was a great help in defending our position.

Written records should include all correspondence, including emails, letters, and even text messages or messages sent through an instant message system. Instruct all of your employees who deal with your partner to sort their messages and then make backups of those messages on a regular basis.

Making Friends

In writing this section on friendship, I want to point out how making friends can be a great help to your partnership. The danger in doing this is that it might sound opportunistic like the only reason to make friends is to help your business. We probably have dealt with people who you know only wanted to be your friend when they saw an advantage to it. In reality that type of a relationship is not a friendship at all and should not be defined as such. When I talk about friendships, I am talking about a true friendship that is built on the fact that the two people genuinely like each other. The benefits to the partnership are a bonus.

Developing friendships between partners should be a natural extension of the two companies working together. You shouldn't make friends just because it is good for business, and you shouldn't tell your employees to be friends with someone either. However, you can encourage them to see if they can find friends among those they work with. You can plan informal gatherings between the two companies where everyone can get to know each other outside the work environment. You can also be a good host when people from the partner company visit.

In any business relationship it is easier for both groups to work together if they actually like each other. It is a good idea to get to know the people who work for your partner company. Friendships help to create a stronger bond between people. It also helps encourage communication and increases the overall well-being of the team members because they like working with each other. If you have a friendship with your counterpart at your partner company, you both will likely try to work through difficult situations. This can be very important particularly in the beginning of a project where there is a lot to learn about working with each other.

Making friends with your partner company's employees will help to make the whole partnership work better. I remember a situation where we had a project with a partner company that ran into a serious problem. We had hired a top-notch programmer to work on the project, and about three months into the project he quit, and we were left holding the bag. In most situations like this, the project would be canceled, and not only would we not have the work but we would also likely have to return some of the money that we were given.

I called my friend at our partner company and explained the situation to him. It put him in a very bad position because he had recommended us for the job and they stood to lose a major partner of their own if the project was not finished on time. Despite all of this, he went out on a limb and gave us the chance to start over again. It was a long, hard process for both of us, but one in which we both grew a lot and even improved our friendship.

I often find that friendships forged through adversity are usually stronger and deeper than those that are a product of surface relationships in normal business. Not that you need to go out and have some rough times to get a few good friends, but rather that when hard times come it is easier to see who your real friends are. I've been through a few rough places and those who believed in me then are the people that I tend to want to work with when times are good.

Long Term Friends

I've found that over the years some of my best friends are people that I have worked with in companies that I have partnered with. These friendships have lasted not only years but decades. The friendships I have made not only were helpful to me in my business but there were a number of times when they gave me the opportunity to help others. Let me give you a couple of examples.

A number of years ago I had the pleasure of working with a major company in our industry. At that company I met an individual (we'll call him Bob) and developed a friendship with him. We corresponded a lot during the course of the project, and not all of it was about business. We talked about our families and hobbies. We talked about life, religion, politics, and the state of the economy. Eventually the project ended and our two companies went their separate ways.

A few years later Bob contacted me. He had left the company and was starting his own company. He remembered visiting my company and was impressed with our organization. He wanted to know if I could give him some pointers and advice about starting his own company. We again corresponded over a period of time; he asking questions and me answering as best I could. He ended up launching his own successful company.

Bob and I kept in touch. He moved to a new city. When I traveled there Bob and I would get together for a visit or meet for a meal. We always made a point of looking each other up at industry conventions.

As time passed I started another company. I contacted Bob and told him about my new venture. He needed some work done and my new company was just the fit for what he needed, so we worked together on a project. He got a project done and I got some much needed business for my new company.

More time passed, and my company had just landed a major project. I had enough local staff to complete most of the project but one part was a real problem. I remembered that Bob had some experience in the area that I needed help with, so I gave him a call and worked out a deal for his company to complete the work we needed.

As you can see, even though our companies changed there were a number of times that Bob and I had a chance to work together. That is the way things are in business. Even though there might be big corporations and they may seem impersonal, those companies are made up of people, and most of the time I have found them to be good people.

Another example is a friend that I made while working in a partnership with one of the biggest companies in our industry. (We will call this friend Jill.) Jill was the head of a division of the company that dealt primarily with helping other companies to be successful using their hardware and software. I made a special effort to be friends with Jill not just because she was in an important position but also because she was (and still is) a good person.

Whenever possible I would make an effort to contact Jill at conventions and other functions. She would always ask me about my family and I would ask her about hers. Although we might go for months without running into each other, we always kept in touch.

Eventually it came time for me to leave the company I had founded and start a new company. In the new direction I wanted to take my company, I saw that it was critical that we work with Jill's company's hardware. Typically, it would take an unknown company months (or more) to get approval to work on their hardware. Because I had an existing relationship with Jill, I gave her a call and she approved us over the phone. It was an incredible opportunity for my new company.

One of the things you don't want to be is a fair weather friend. If you can't learn to like a person for the person he or she is, you are better off just keeping business relationships to business and not looking for anything deeper. People can tell when your friendship is genuine and when it is not. If the only time you contact someone is when you want to sell them something, you will never gain a true friend. To gain a true friend, you need to be able to take an interest in the person, not just the business position that person holds. This takes a lot of informal communication. Communication that has nothing to do with business but a lot to do with the person you are talking with.

Deliver on Promises

If any promises are made to your partner, and there almost always are, make sure you deliver on those promises. Promises can include things like meeting a deadline or delivering a product on time. It can also mean keeping something confidential or helping to promote a product to the public. Almost anything can be viewed as a promise if it is important to your partner and you committed to do it.

Contractual Promises

The most vital promises are those that are part of any contract or agreement that you sign with your partner. Everyone at your company should give those promises their highest priority. Make sure that those responsible for performing on those contract points not only understand them but understand why they are important.

A good practice with any contract or agreement is to go through it carefully and make a list of all your company obligations. Those that have delivery dates should also include those dates on the list. This list will come in very handy for you and your managers as you work to perform your part of the agreement. For those in your company who only have responsibility for a portion of the list, you can create smaller sub-lists.

Contractual promises are important for your partnership. The reason that they are included in the agreement between your two companies is that they probably formed the basis of the partnership to begin with. When they are written into a contract they become legally binding. This means that if your company does not perform its duties as outlined in the contract there can be legal consequences.

It is highly likely that as a business owner you already understand the importance of living up to contractual promises. These promises are spelled out clearly on paper, and in most cases, once they are down on paper they are expected. In addition to contractual promises, there are also a number of informal promises that are also important to honor.

Be on Time

Time is a critical element for most large businesses. Although to the small business owner the large company may seem like a slow moving object, the important thing is that it does move. It takes a lot more effort to move something big than it does to move something small. When something slows or stops a large object from moving, it takes some time to get it going again. That is why it is so important to meet all of your time critical commitments when working with a large company, including being on time to all your appointments.

In a small company, if you are late to a meeting you may annoy a half dozen people. Being late to a meeting at a large company could mean wasting the time of thousands of people and costing the company a lot of money. It isn't just the people in the meeting; it affects all of the people who are waiting for those in the meeting to get done so that they can continue their work. Let's consider an example.

John calls a meeting of his plant managers to show them your new product that will speed the process of manufacturing. The meeting is scheduled for 2:00 PM. The plant managers arrive on time but you are half an hour late, and the meeting subsequently lasts a half hour longer. Several of the plant managers had other meetings scheduled after your meeting. These meetings all get pushed back. In a couple of cases, problems back at the plant are causing production to be halted until they can contact the plant manager who is tied up in your meeting. Not only did your being late reflect poorly on your product, but it cost the company significantly in a number of other areas as well.

Punctuality is the hallmark of efficiency. Large companies put a premium on efficiency in both their operations and in their personnel. They are constantly looking for ways to be more efficient. By being on time to every meeting, you will improve your standing with your partner. In addition to being on time, be prepared.

As a general rule, the larger the company the greater the potential problems might be if you don't keep your schedule commitments. Larger organizations have more moving parts and work on a larger scale. They need to have things on schedule or it costs them a significant amount of money and lost productivity.

One of the toughest businesses to try to keep to a production schedule is software development. In this business, you can plan and work to get everything to come together on time only to have one software bug totally throw off your project. If you want an example, just look at how many times products like Microsoft Windows operating systems are delayed or how many times the release date of a highly anticipated video game gets pushed back.

We were given a huge opportunity once from one of our partners to create a high-profile product for them. Everything went well up until we were trying to finish the product. We had everything working in the product, but there was a random crash bug that we just couldn't find. It delayed the product by more than a month. Our partner had to delay shipping the product and lost millions in the process.

Sometimes no matter how well you plan, problems occur that cause delays in a project. These delays can not only have financial consequences, they can also reflect negatively on your company. We all may find ourselves wanting to please our partner and deliver on a tight deadline but be careful because, if you miss, it could ruin everything you worked for to get the partnership in the first place. If the schedule is a problem, make sure you deal with it upfront. The general rule of underpromise and overdeliver works best.

In the last several chapters we have given much thought to the fact that the larger the corporation the slower things happen and the less likely there will be any rapid changes. Large companies are like large moving objects. They develop inertia and it is difficult to change their course. Anything that disturbs that course can be seen as a problem. This includes not having something on schedule. For a large organization to run smoothly, it has to have everything work on a schedule.

In a smaller organization there usually isn't as much of a problem if something comes in a little late or early, usually accommodations can be made. However, in a large company something not happening when it is supposed to can set off a chain reaction that can cause major problems. This is because everything is in such a large scale. For example, a small company may order 10,000 boxes to package its new product. The smaller company has everyone pitch in and stuff the boxes when the order comes in, taking about a week to get them all ready for market. A larger company contemplating the same thing may make an order of 1,000,000 boxes.

There is a big magnitude difference between 10,000 boxes and 1,000,000 boxes. To get 1,000,000 boxes ready to ship to the retail market, the company has to have a system for getting the products in the boxes and then getting the boxes to market. There are warehousing costs, packaging costs, shipping costs, and much more. Typically larger companies will hire a significant number of people to deal just with the packaging and delivery of goods. Running the whole operation can be very costly and very complicated. If something isn't delivered on time, the whole operation grinds to a halt and a significant amount of money is wasted. If your company is the reason for the waste, you can bet there will be problems with your partnership.

Company Rules

Large companies often develop a corporate rulebook with mandates regarding how employees dress and how they act. Some companies will actually have written guidelines for employees to follow, which the employee receives on the first day on the job. A company's rules are important; they do this for protection and for image. Rules of conduct help keep employees and companies out of trouble. Large companies often find themselves the target of lawsuits. Many times these lawsuits are brought on because of the actions of someone within the corporation.

Lawsuits seem to be about anything these days. Some of these lawsuits are legitimate and serve a vital purpose in society, but many seem to be more about getting money, rather than any desire for justice. Because lawsuits have become so prevalent in recent times, many companies have very strict guidelines for their employees to try to make sure they minimize any reason for lawsuit.

Even though your company is a separate organization, when you are acting in concert with your larger partner, it is a good idea to respect their rules and to go along with them. It's not uncommon for the public to mistake employees of a partner company for those of the larger company. For this reason alone it is a good idea to respect your partner company's rules and act accordingly. You can explain all you want to customers that you are from a different company, but the mere fact that you are working with the larger company means there is a connection.

Company Culture

Over time companies develop their own culture. This is true no matter what size the company might be. I remember talking with a former IBM employee about how not only was he expected to wear a tie to work but there were specific kinds of ties that were acceptable and others that were not. As he explained it to me, IBM had a very specific culture that was maintained throughout the entire company. Of course, that was years ago and the company may have changed. The important thing to note is how your partner company's culture matches up to yours.

If your company has a loose, open culture where employees come and go as they want and are only required to put in a certain amount of time at work every week, and your partner keeps strict company work schedules, you may find that there is a communication problem between the two companies. An even bigger danger comes if employees from both companies are to work on the same site.

Company culture is developed by the management style of the company and how the employees react to that style. You may have heard of the open, progressive management style of companies like Apple and Google where they emphasize creativity and innovation rather than strict work hours. In both these companies the management specifically wanted the employees to work in a stimulating and creative environment. To create this feeling they developed a management style that encouraged creative thought. The company culture was an outgrowth of how the employees reacted to the management style.

Some companies have found that their company culture can become a positive public aspect of their company. For example, if a company culture includes having all of their employees greet everyone with a smile and a hello, they will be perceived by the public as a friendly company. If the company culture includes employees going out of their way to help customers to resolve any problem they may have, the company will be perceived as being helpful.

Mandated customer appreciation doesn't always work. A few years ago Kmart was dealing with the ever-increasing competition from Wal-Mart. To become more competitive, Kmart management decided that they needed to have their employees be more friendly and courteous to their customers. They implemented a plan where they asked all their employees to memorize the words "Thank You For Shopping At Kmart." They even printed the initials T. Y. F. S. A. K. near the cash registers to remind them what to say. While just saying thank you was a nice gesture, it didn't have the effect they wanted, because thankfulness isn't just words; it is an emotional state. If employees don't really care to be thankful, it doesn't work.

The point here is that just because someone from your partner company tells you what the company culture is in your contract negotiations, it doesn't necessarily mean that it is truly what they say. You need to see it for yourself to be certain.

Having different company cultures doesn't mean that the two companies can't work well as partners. It just means that the two companies need to be aware of the cultural differences as part of understanding each other.

Don't Poach

If there is one sure way to end a partnership very quickly it is for one company to entice an employee from the other company. *Poaching*, as it is sometimes referred to, is when a company with inside knowledge entices key employees to leave their current employer and come to work for them. A partnership situation is particularly susceptible to this problem because both companies get an inside peek at their partner company and learn which employees are the real stars.

Usually the danger of losing employees is greater for the smaller of the partners because the larger company has more opportunities with which to entice an employee. However, I've seen a number of occasions where the smaller company does pull in a key employee from the larger company. It usually results in the end of the partnership and in some situations it can even result in legal proceedings, especially when trade secrets are involved.

The best way to deal with poaching is to write an agreement in the contract that precludes either party from hiring someone from the other company without prior written consent of the company where the employee is currently working.

In some situations the employee may approach you without any provocation on your part. In most cases the best course is to point out the non-hire clause and let them know you legally can't hire them without permission first. This will usually take care of the problem, however, sometimes it makes sense for the person to come work for your company. For example, maybe your company is located closer to where the person wants to live. Maybe their skill set would be better suited to your company. Maybe they are unhappy working for a large company and want to work for a smaller company. You also might want to check to see if the employee has a non-compete clause in their employee agreement. Because you are likely in the same industry, the non-compete clause will preclude them from working for your company until it expires.

If you think it will be a good business move for you to hire someone from your partner company, you need to have an open discussion with your partner first. This conversation should only happen if you and the potential employee are both committed to the change of employment. Either you or the employee can bring it up with your partner company, but in no case should you just take their word for it. You should always speak directly with their supervisor to see how the shift in employment might be viewed.

In some cases your partner company may agree with the change in employment and there will be no problem. No company wants someone working for them who really would rather work somewhere else. In other cases they will disagree with it. If you have given your word not to take any of their employees, then you should walk away from the opportunity to hire the employee no matter how tempting it might be. The reputation that you poach employees will get around and you may find yourself with no potential partners in the future because other companies have heard that you do not honor your commitments.

Even if you have no formal agreement with the company, it is still a good idea to never hire an employee from your partner company without first talking to the company and receiving their blessing. If there is any indication of displeasure from your partner company, you must think long and hard about making the hire. In almost every situation, you are better off not hiring the person.

Keep It Win/Win

A good relationship in business is one that benefits both parties. When the relationships are win/win, they tend to last longer and are more beneficial overall than relationships that favor one party over the other. Over time the nature of a relationship can change, however, making it less beneficial to one or the other partner. To keep the partnership win/win you need to review the partnership regularly.

After a partnership is in place and working for a period of time, it is often tempting to change things to help benefit your company. These changes might seem reasonable but they can have an adverse effect on your partner. For example, you might want to change personnel because some of your better employees who are working on the partnership might be more useful to you in another project. Placing a less experienced person on the partnership project might seem okay because the project is running smoothly and you really do need someone good on this other project, but it could create a problem. You should always think carefully when moving personnel, especially if you have made commitments to your partner on the people who will work on the project. Let me give you an example.

I was once in the role of the larger company contracting work out to a new programming group that was just starting. We knew the group and had a high level of trust in their abilities. We thought we could give them a hand to get them started and gave them a key role in one of our projects. After several months, though, things seemed to not be going as well as we hoped. Some investigation uncovered that a few months into the project they landed a bigger deal with another company. Because they felt the other deal was more important than our project, they hired some programmers who had no real experience to work on our project. The end result was that they did fine on their bigger deal but our project was a total disaster. It was a very bitter pill for us, one that took us a few years to recover from.

We learned from that experience to always specify in our contract who the team members will be on any future contracts. I also learned why our larger partners wanted the same from us and why they often want to inspect our offices and see for themselves who will be working on our project. Part of the reason that a project runs smoothly is directly attributable to the people who are working on the partnership. Changing the people working on a partnership will change how it is working. Sometimes when it isn't working well changes have to be made, but when a project is working well changes will likely have a negative effect on it. This is particularly true when you are replacing more experienced people with those who have less experience.

A win/win attitude in business is when you place as much emphasis on the well-being of your partner as you do your own company. This means that you consider how any changes you make to your staff might affect them. Will it impact their portion of the partnership? What will that impact be?

Win/win in business is really like the Golden Rule in life. Treat your partner as you want them to treat you. It is really just common sense. If your partner is happy with how things are going, they will likely want to continue with the partnership.

Why is it so important to look at how things will affect your partner? It all comes down to taking a longer term view of your business goals and objectives. Something that is sorely lacking in business today is the idea of long term reputations. In a way, it goes back to our second topic in this chapter—integrity. Short term decisions have long term ramifications. If you make a choice today that hurts or negatively affects you partnership, you are also negatively affecting the lives of the people who work for your partner. And believe me, those people will remember.

You never know what twists of fate will bring people in and out of your life. Junior managers become senior managers, often at different companies. Decisions you make today can and often do come back to haunt you. In the normal course of business you will make enough mistakes without doing something that you know will hurt your partner's business. You don't need to add more negative feelings to your reputation.

When you look out for the best interests of your partner, in most cases you are also looking out for the best interests of your own company. I remember a situation where we had a major project that our company was working through. We had formed a partnership with another company to help us get the work completed. During the course of development we ran into a major snag with the hardware. It just didn't have the performance capabilities that we needed to have a competitive product. As we were evaluating our options, our partner came to us with a possible solution. Because of the nature of the project there was no extra money in it for development of new technology. However, their approach was so novel that we created another agreement to move forward with their technology in the hopes of not only exploiting our current product but several others beyond it.

After a few months of joint work in which both companies invested considerable effort, money, and time, the new technology was ready. It was so successful that it completely changed our product and made it infinitely better than it was before. It turned failure into success.

Our partner company could have just walked away from the project. They could have also exploited their idea on their own. Instead they opted to continue to work with us in the face of great financial strain. Needless to say, they moved to the top of our list of partners for future projects.

Change with the Times

In today's world, business moves much faster than it once did. Not only is technology advancing at an incredible rate, but methods of communication and business deals are changing continually. Companies seem to grow and die faster than they used to. In many industries, shifts in consumer demand seem to be happening faster and faster. The problem with all of this fast movement is that without some sort of flexibility in your partnership, you may find that the original goals of your partnership are impossible to reach.

There are two very important reasons why your partnership should be flexible enough to change with the times. The first is to make sure that the partnership remains profitable for both you and your partner. The second is to take advantage of opportunities to build an even better partnership.

Remain Profitable

The business landscape is an ever-changing environment. Consumer buying trends tend to change significantly from year to year. Something that was popular a few years ago ends up on the clearance racks today. Take, for example, the recent shifts in the new car market. In 2008 when gas peaked at $4.50 per gallon, large pick-up and SUV sales took a hard nose dive. Used car lots were filled to capacity with these huge metal behemoths and new car sales for SUVs and large pick-ups were almost nonexistent. It was a major crisis for the U.S. auto industry, which relied heavily on the sales of larger vehicles.

The gas price spike was soon followed by one of the worst economic recessions in recent memory, so when gas prices fell, the U.S. auto industry was faced with arguably its biggest crisis ever. Two of the major car makers—General Motors and Chrysler—had to borrow money from the government and both had to later declare bankruptcy. Not only were large automobiles not selling, nothing was selling because consumers couldn't get auto loans and most simply didn't want to spend money when they were worried about keeping their jobs.

During the gas price spike, fuel efficient cars were selling as fast as they could be made, but once the recession hit even they were difficult to move. This time was one of intense turmoil and tough choices for not only the U.S.

automakers but other car companies as well. It was a time of extreme shifts in consumer buying practices.

During this time, however, one car company made significant gains because they were nimble and saw a way to take advantage of the economic situation. Hyundai came out with a program that let the buyers of their cars return them with no adverse effect to the buyer's credit if they found they couldn't afford the payment due to poor economic conditions. This simple program gave car buyers some security that enabled them to go ahead and buy a Hyundai car even in the face of an uncertain future. The program was a big success for Hyundai and enabled them to increase sales during a time when every other car maker was taking big losses. By working together with your partners, you may be able to do the same when faced with a market challenge.

The preceding story underscores the need to be able to make changes for the benefit of a partnership. Something that made sense a few months ago may just not be feasible today. In the face of this quick-paced, ever-changing environment that we all face as business owners, we have to find ways to change the nature of a partnership to keep it from becoming a drain on one or the other company.

Let's take a look at a situation in which a small lumber company has made a partnership with a furniture manufacturer to supply raw lumber for the building of fine furniture. Shortly after the partnership is made, new environmental regulations are passed by Congress that change the way lumber of hardwoods can be extracted from forests. These changes not only drive up the cost of harvesting lumber, they also make it more difficult for the lumber company to meet its deadlines with its current equipment and staff.

The lumber company has a contract and is obligated to fulfill the contract regardless of the effect of the new rules. The furniture company could enforce the contract and require the wood at the given price, but the result would be devastating to the lumber company. In this situation, by enforcing the contract the furniture company runs the risk of losing a valuable long term partner. If, on the other hand, the furniture company recognizes the problem and works out a compromise with the lumber company, they stand to have the continued support of a partner that can supply them with lumber for the long term.

By taking advantage of the partnership in the short term, the furniture company will get cheaper lumber and possibly a short term sales advantage over its competition, but it will also cause the lumber company to go out of business. By working with the lumber company and helping them through the changing lumber harvesting regulations, the furniture company may have to raise its own prices, but it is highly likely that the entire furniture industry will have to do the same eventually anyway. However, the longer term advantage could go to the furniture company in that it has secured a steady stream of lumber for years to come at what will likely be a better price than what it could negotiate with a new supplier.

There are a number of ways to make a partnership flexible even within a contractual agreement by placing language in it that allows either party to request a change in the contract based on a change in the scope of work required. But even if no such language exists, there should be openness between partners to address needed changes whenever they occur, especially if the adverse effects to the one of the companies are severe.

We had a situation with a publisher once where the market for the product we were producing for them had changed. There was also some difficulty getting our product to market. We saw that the publisher was standing to lose money. We had a meeting with them to discuss possible solutions to the problem. What came out of the meeting was that we would create for them an additional product that they could sell and hopefully make up for the loss in revenue they were going to have from the first product.

What we stood to gain from the new deal was that we got to choose the product, and that gave us an opportunity to build a product around some intellectual property that we controlled introducing it to the market. We also gained goodwill from the publisher and an opportunity to develop more products with them. The publisher got another product without having to lay out the development costs. All in all, it worked out for both groups.

Opportunities

Instead of looking at changes in partnerships as just a defensive mechanism for keeping both companies profitable, it should also be viewed as a way for both companies to prosper. The difference here is one of opportunity rather than expediency.

The forces that bring you together for a partnership are the same forces that can bring greater opportunities for both your company and your partner company. The significant difference after you become partners is that you both gain insight into each company. This means that if there are reasons to partner with each other before you really get to know each other, there should be even more reasons to partner after you get to know each other.

Depending on the type of partnership you form, you should think of your partner as an extension of your own company. The advantage of that type of thinking is that you can expand your opportunities to include those that are on the same level as your partner company. In other words, instead of just looking at what your company can do, learn what your partner can do and then think of what you can do together.

Know When to Say When

No partnership will last forever. Even the best partnership will run its course and need to end. When this happens it is always better to know how to gracefully step away from the partnership and move on.

At one point, we had a partnership with a company that was supplying the majority of our work. As time progressed, we saw a chance to change directions and significantly increase the size of projects that our company was fulfilling. We tried to continue to serve our client while going in a different direction, but it soon become apparent that it just wasn't going to work anymore, because we needed the resources to work on our new contracts. I called our client and explained the situation to him. In addition, I also found another company that needed the work and could do a good job for them. We worked out a timeframe for phasing out their work and transferring to the new company.

The key points when ending a partnership are to talk frankly with your partner and let them know you intend to end the partnership. Together you can work out a plan for an ordered and pleasant transition. If possible, supply for them an alternate group or company that can continue the work. If you follow this procedure, you can end the partnership and still be on good terms with the company.

Not every partnership will work out well. Some will have problems that just make them impractical to continue. As a business owner, it is important that you understand when to end the partnership and when not to. I have seen instances where partnerships were ended too soon and those where they should have ended long before they did. With the perspective of hindsight it is always easy to second guess what would have been the best course of action, but when dealing with the present, there are a few warning signs that might indicate a partnership needs to be terminated.

Unprofitable

One of the major reasons to end a partnership is when the partnership has become unprofitable. If a partnership is unprofitable, it is also likely that you are taking a loss on the project. Even if the project is just breaking even, that is enough reason to end the relationship. Unprofitable projects can become drains on company resources and are problematic because the resources devoted to the unprofitable project could be diverted toward a more successful endeavor.

When a project becomes unprofitable, there are a few things that you should do prior to ending the partnership. First, you need to take a look at the project and see if it is likely to remain unprofitable or if it can become profitable with additional effort. For example, often projects or systems are unprofitable in the beginning because the team is learning how to do the work. Given time the process becomes easier to handle and the project becomes more profitable. Will a management change help the project to become more profitable? Look at where the costs are going and see if changes can be made to bring the project back into profitability.

You can't always just look at a profit and loss statement to determine profitability. These statements are just snapshots of a given time period and don't look at the overall life cycle of a project. Sometimes the profits for a project are recognized at the end of the project when the product goes to market. The project might be unprofitable now but it may be very profitable once the product hits the market. Other times the major money in a contract might not come until much of the work is done. In these cases, the project has to be viewed as a whole and not on a daily profit report. A project might be unprofitable now but very profitable once all of the money is received.

To give an example on a very small scale, I go back to when I was just starting my graphics business shortly after graduating college. I took on a project with a company that had a lot of continuous work. Because I was new to the field, my initial attempts at the work paid very poorly. I was actually making more money on my other projects, but I felt that if I stuck with it, I could learn the skill and eventually make the work profitable. The advantage of the new work was that I didn't have to spend as much time looking for business and could devote more time to doing billable work. I looked at the learning curve as an investment in the new partnership. As time passed and I learned the new skills I needed to complete the projects for my new partner, I got better and better at the work required. What seemed at first to be unprofitable work became my most profitable work.

Is the relationship with the partner more important than immediate profitability? Sometimes it is worth the effort to complete an unprofitable project as a way to open doors to more profitable projects in the future. Building a relationship with a major company might be worth some initial pain if that relationship turns into something that gives your company an edge for better projects in the future.

Are there other things that the company gains from the project beyond profit? For example, the company may enter into a partnership to gain better community relations. Maybe there are political reasons for continuing the partnership. Maybe you are looking to establish business in a new market area and this project helps with that. Maybe the project is high profile and has a great chance in giving your company much needed publicity. Take a look at the total benefits to the partnership. If you have to, convert all the benefits into what you would have to pay for them so you can measure everything together on the same scale. When you have a complete picture of all benefits to the partnership, you can make a better decision.

Less Profitable

Less profitable is similar to unprofitable, but not as critical from a time standpoint. You may be able to live with a less profitable project, but you are endangering your company if you choose to do an unprofitable project.

In the case of a less profitable project you aren't losing money, you just aren't making as much money as you could be. In this situation, it is often better to let the partnership run its course and then just not renew it when it is over. If the partnership is open-ended, you might have to set a date with your partner for when you will want the current arrangement to end.

As companies grow and progress, they will often find that a partnership that made sense a year ago doesn't make sense this year. For example, your company might have grown to the point that the project is just too small to warrant your current company size. Small projects tend to have as much management time and effort as large projects.

Maybe you have a better partnership opportunity and it will be successful only if you have staff available to do it. In this case, you should be honest with your partner and explain why you are no longer interested in a partnership with them. Whatever you do, though, don't understaff a project or put unqualified people on it just because it isn't as profitable as your other projects. It is better to end the partnership than underperform on it.

Payment Problems

Some partnerships may look good on paper but when you get into the actual partnership you find the money just isn't coming when it is supposed to. Even though you should be making a decent profit off the work you find that because the payments are delayed or you aren't paid on time you are running at a deficit.

Usually payment problems indicate that there are other problems in the company you are working with. This is a big red flag and you should consider it carefully. You can't survive if you don't get paid. If they are paying slowly, they are holding on to your money. You are likely in other partnerships in which you are obligated to pay on time; you need to make sure you have some a good cash flow. You might need to consider ending the partnership before you run the risk of having cash problems yourself.

Incompatibility

Not all partnerships will work. Sometimes there are such cultural or management differences between the two companies that it creates an impossible situation. If your employees are constantly complaining about your partner and how they are treated, you may need to end the partnership or face severe problems in your own company.

I remember one partner we had who would call our employees at any time of day or night and expect them to jump on whatever they needed right then. At first our employees tried to accommodate our partner, but eventually the problem grew so great that they told me that would rather quit than continue working with them. Although the project was bringing in good business for our company, we opted to end the partnership rather than risk losing some of our most valuable employees.

More Than You Can Handle

There are times when a partnership may be just too much for your company. This can happen when things are going well and your partner scales up the project beyond your capacity. It can also happen when you have unknowingly landed a partnership in which you don't have the right expertise, or in the case where a key employee leaves your company. In these cases you are better off being upfront with your partner and explaining the situation. A bad partnership is worse than no partnership.

Change in Direction

Your company may need to make a change in its business strategy. Maybe for economic reasons or for the sake of finding a better market, you decide to change how or what your company produces. Because of the change in direction, the current partnership may no longer make sense. In this case, it is much better for you to end the partnership and focus on what your company needs to do rather than continue to do work that no longer moves your company in the direction it needs to go.

A good example is a company that creates software for its partner companies. Maybe they started out focusing on user interfaces and as the company grew they became more involved in databases and application development. If their original partnerships were with other application development companies, there will likely be ample reason to end those partnerships because the company now competes with them.

Change in Management or Company Status

At some point you may no longer be the boss or your company may need to be shut down. It could just be that you want to retire or you may need to close the company because it is no longer viable. In these situations, existing partnerships are likely to be impractical or impossible to continue.

Always Talk First

No matter what the problem might be, you should always have a frank discussion with your partner before you end the relationship. No problem is insurmountable. Too often a company will just throw up their hands and walk away. They never give the partner, which they worked so hard to gain, a chance to fix the issues.

If there is an argument, give yourself time to cool down and look at the problem objectively. If there are hurt feelings, see if an apology or some other solution might be available. If there are financial issues, make them known and see if there is a way to work through them.

Can you go to your partner and renegotiate a better deal? Don't just assume that your partner will not change the terms of your agreement. Before you kill the partnership, ask. It won't hurt, and you might just walk away with something that works for your company while retaining a valuable partner.

You worked hard for the partnership. Don't throw it away unless you are sure it is the only solution. Remember that partnerships have a lot more value than just money to your company. Review why you went into the partnership in the first place and see if those reasons still make sense for your company.

In the end, if the partnership no longer makes sense or the problem outweighs the benefits you may just need to dissolve it and move on. This is never an easy decision, but ultimately a bad partnership is not going to help either company.

Making Partnerships Work for You

In this chapter we have attempted to give you some good information to help you through the performance side of your partnership. While it is impossible to cover every aspect of how to run a good partnership in one chapter, we have compiled what we hope will be helpful to you as you move forward with your partnership.

In the end, if you want a partnership to work you have to work on the partnership. It is like any relationship: it will only be as good as the effort you and your partner put into it. Hard work and honesty will make up for a lot of mistakes.

If you ever run into a problem that you just can't solve, take a look at some of your community resources. There are often business clubs or organizations that have a number of small and large business owners who meet on a regular basis. These groups are a wealth of information, and you can often build relationships with people who have already faced the problems you are dealing with. A few well-placed questions can bring you amazing insights.

As a whole there are a lot more business opportunities out there for small business owners than you may realize. Having the courage and know-how to make partnerships with larger companies can bring significant rewards to you and your company. Our hope in writing this book is to give you a resource that will help you through the process. While it may sometimes seem complex and daunting, the rewards can be great.

Index

DISCARD